40 DAYS
DEVOTIONAL
JOURNAL

Therese Marszalek

40 Days Devotional Journal
ISBN: 978-1-936314-81-2
© 2013 by Therese Marszalek
PO Box 668
Nine Mile Falls, WA 99026

therese.marszalek@gmail.com
www.theresemarszalek.com

Published by Word and Spirit Publishing
P.O. Box 701403
Tulsa, Oklahoma 74170

DEDICATION

I dedicate this devotional journal to my dear friend and sister in Christ, Joanne Brunskill, owner of Celebrate Your Faith*. You are one of my most beloved DOTS and I thank God for connecting us with His divine purpose. Thank you, Joanne, for believing in and supporting the ministry to which God called me. Thank you and Rick for your generosity in providing a place of seclusion in Sedona for me to complete this work. I admire your unwavering faith and passionate pursuit of our awesome God. You and Rick are a gift to me and to the body of Christ. When I grow up I want to be like you as you remind me of someone I know: His name is Jesus. I bless you, love you and thank God that we will have eternity to catch up.

To Diane!
Bless you
you're one of my
favorite DOTS!
So glad we're on this
journey with Jesus together!
Love you!
Debbie Morphew

* Celebrate Your Faith (www.celebrateyourfaith.com) connects people to God and offers an extraordinary collection of handcrafted artisan gifts, jewelry, Bibles and home décor from around the world. .

MESSAGE FROM THE AUTHOR

Many, as I experienced, know Jesus as Lord and Savior, know the Holy Spirit as Counselor and friend, but for various reasons have never understood or known the love of Father God as a loving Father. This 40-day journaling journey will pave the way for a deeper intimacy with the Father. My five-year wilderness journey to the Father's love is documented in my previous book *From the Wilderness to the Miraculous* (Destiny Image). Knowing the love of the Father changed me forever. I encourage you to read *From the Wilderness to the Miraculous* to gain a better understanding of the wondrous miracles and transformation that can result from times in the wilderness, where I found the wondrous love of the Father.

40 Days Devotional Journal is a companion to my most recent book, *40 Days: Inspiration & Encouragement to Get You Through Tough Times* (Word and Spirit Publishing). Although you can use this devotional journal by itself, I recommend using it in conjunction with *40 Days* at it contains anointed devotionals that magnify the messages of each day.

Prophetically, the number 40 represents the wilderness. After being delivered from Egypt under the bondage of a heavy-handed slave driver, the nation of Israel wandered for 40 challenging years in the wilderness on a journey to the Promised Land. Jesus, after His baptism in the river Jordan, was sent *by the Holy Spirit* into the wilderness, where for 40 days, He endured intense testing and temptation. Maybe you, like Jesus, were sent into a God ordained wilderness season where you've faced intense temptation and testing. Or, like Israel, you've been navigating through a wilderness season, trying to get freed from an Egyptian type bondage where you've encountered challenges.

Weary wilderness travelers cover the globe. Whatever the reasons for which you've found yourself in the wilderness, you're perfectly positioned for a new season of revival where you will be supernaturally strengthened body, soul and spirit by your wilderness guide: Father God, who IS love (1 John 4:8).

God had a divinely orchestrated purpose and plan for Jesus' and Israel's time in the wilderness. He created a divinely orchestrated plan and purpose for you too, one that was set in motion before you ever set foot on the earth.

It is my prayer that you will emerge from this 40-day experience as Jesus emerged from His 40 days of wilderness - in the *power* of the Holy Spirit, and as Israel emerged from 40 years in the wilderness — in the Promised Land of God's blessings. As our heavenly Father draws you by His Spirit and transforms you by the power of His love, may you never be the same again.

HOW TO USE 40 DAYS DEVOTIONAL JOURNAL

Set apart 40 consecutive days that you can dedicate to completing the journaling journey. Ideally, choose a location to meet with God daily, preferably a place free from interruptions and distractions. Before you start each day, quiet yourself and come freely before the Lord knowing that He is delighted in meeting with you. If you become aware of distracting thoughts about your pending to-do list, make note of them and set it aside to tend to later. This is your time with Father God. Everything else can wait.

GIVE THANKS

Psalm 100:4 says, "Enter His gates with thanksgiving and His courts with praise; give thanks to Him and praise His Name." (NIV) Express your thanks to the Father and record your thanks in the space provided.

MEDITATION

Read the meditation of the day, ponder what it means to you personally and then meditate on it throughout the day. Speak the meditation out loud. The words you speak today provide the framework for your tomorrow so build a strong framework on which God will build. May your meditation be pleasing to Him, as you rejoice in the Lord. (Psalm 104:34)

SCRIPTURE FOCUS

Read the scripture focus verse(s) and look it up in your Bible, consulting other Bible versions if desired for greater understanding. Read verses

before and after focus verse for extra study. Allow the Holy Spirit to speak to you through the Scriptures. If you are using *40 Days* (Word and Spirit Books) on your journey, read the devotion for the day.

REFLECTION

Four reflection questions are followed by space to journal your responses. Ask the Holy Spirit to help you search your heart and allow Him to take you to places where you'll find healing and revelation. As you listen and respond to what He reveals, document your thoughts. Reflect on what He is saying, for the Lord will give you insight into all this. (2 Tim 2:7)

REPENTANCE

Acts 3:19 says, "Repent then, and turn to God, so that your sins may be wiped out, that times of refreshing may come from the Lord." Read the prayer of repentance and add additional areas of repentance as the Holy Spirit brings conviction to your heart. As you confess your sins, He is faithful and just and will forgive your sins, and purify you of all unrighteousness. (1 John 1:9)

SUBMISSION

James 4:7 says, "Submit yourself, then, to God." As you submit yourself wholly to Him, and allow Him to have His way in your life, He will lead you to His abundant life in the Promised Land of His blessings. Read the prayer of submission, then journal other areas of submission God brings to mind.

FROM THE FATHER'S HEART

Read the Father's message and receive it personally. Ask the Holy Spirit to open your spiritual ears to hear the Father's voice. As the prophet Samuel said, "Speak, Lord, for your servant is listening." (1 Samuel 3:9) Liberal space is included to journal what the Father speaks to your heart.

This section is a key part of your journey to know Father God's love. The Bible says, "My sheep listen to My voice; I know them and they follow me. (John 10:27, NIV) Know that you hear his voice.

* Sketches are drawn by artist Jan Foland and are part of *The Father's LoveLine,* a greeting card line released by Therese Marszalek Ministries. Cards are available through www.theresemarszalek.com, www.celebrateyourfaith.com and various other locations.

40 DAYS
DEVOTIONAL
JOURNAL

DAY 1

Father, today I'm thankful for:

_____

_____

_____

_____

_____

_____

_____

_____

_____

Meditation

As I fill my heart with God's love, I eliminate available space for fear to take root. On my lifelong journey in Christ, I'm growing daily in my understanding of His love for me. I want to learn my Father's love as He teaches me through His Word and through His personal dealings with me. I submit myself to Him, and insist that fear flee far from me.

May my meditation be pleasing to him, as I rejoice in the LORD.
(Psalm 104:34)

Scripture Focus

Then Jesus said, "Come to me, all of you who are weary
and carry heavy burdens, and I will give you rest."
(Matthew 11:28, NLT)

FOR REFLECTION

1. Schedule at least two hours away with the Lord in a private setting where I will have no disruptions. Be sure to bring a notebook, a pen and an open heart.

   Date and time: _____

   Location: _____

2. Reflect on the burdens that weigh on my heart. Make a list of my burdens.

   _____   _____

   _____   _____

   _____   _____

   _____   _____

   _____   _____

   _____   _____

3. One at a time, talk to my Father about the burdens I have been carrying. Release them, one at a time, into His hands. Describe the experience:

   _____

   _____

   _____

   _____

   _____

   _____

4. Sit quietly before the Lord and receive His rest. Let Him pour into me, filling me to the fullest capacity. Describe the experience.

_____

_____

_____

_____

_____

_____

_____

Reflect on what I am saying, for the Lord will give you insight into all this.
(2 Timothy 2:7)

REPENTANCE

Loving Father, I have taken my relationship with You for granted, turning elsewhere instead of coming to You when I'm weary and burdened. How often I have failed to remember the great price that Your Son paid so that I might come to You. Forgive me for getting sidetracked with the busyness of life and ignoring You when You've summoned me into Your presence. Help me Father, to respond in a way that might be pleasing in Your sight and let me never leave Your presence the same as I arrived.

OTHER AREAS OF REPENTANCE

_____

_____

_____

_____

_____

_____

Repent, then, and turn to God, so that your sins may be wiped out,
that times of refreshing may come from the Lord.
(Acts 3:19)

SUBMISSION

Father God, how I long to be with You. How I long to come away with You for a time of rest and restoration. I offer You my schedules, my agendas and my plans, and ask You to bring divine order to my life, creating regular times of refreshing with You. Lord, I will respond to Your call and will follow where You lead. Here I am, Lord. Have Your way in me. In Jesus' Name.

OTHER AREAS OF SUBMISSION

Submit yourselves, then, to God.
(James 4:7)

FROM THE FATHER'S HEART

My Child, I long to share times of intimacy with you. Even as you sleep, I watch over you and anticipate our next meeting. In the midst of the busyness of your life, I am present and prepared to respond to your every need. Come to Me, My beloved one, give Me your burdens, and I shall give you My rest.

PERSONAL WORD FROM MY FATHER

_____

_____

_____

_____

_____

_____

_____

_____

_____

_____

_____

_____

_____

_____

_____

_____

_____

_____

_____

_____

Speak, LORD, for your servant is listening.
(1 Samuel 3:9)

DAY 2

Father, today I'm thankful for:

_____

_____

_____

_____

_____

_____

_____

_____

_____

_____

_____

Meditation

Regular times of refreshing are necessary to maintain rest in my soul. Daily, I will respond when Jesus says, "Come." Jesus paid a great price to provide me with the privilege of coming into God's presence so I could give Him my burdens and receive His rest.

May my meditation be pleasing to him, as I rejoice in the LORD.
(Psalm 104:34)

Scripture Focus

There is no fear in love. But perfect love drives out fear, because fear has to do with punishment. The one who fears is not made perfect in love.
(1 John 4:18)

FOR REFLECTION

1. Am I confident that my eternity is secure in Christ? On what do I base that confidence?

2. What fears still remain in my life? Make a list of them and talk to the Father about them, allowing adequate time to listen to His personal words to me.

3. Do I believe that God loves me? What hinders me from believing that my heavenly Father loves me unconditionally?

_____

_____

_____

4. What steps can I take to grow in my understanding of God's love? Do I know any people who appear to abide in the peace of God? Ask them to share their journey with me.

_____

_____

_____

_____

_____

_____

Reflect on what I am saying, for the Lord will give you insight into this.
(2 Timothy 2:7)

REPENTANCE

Holy Father, I have been gripped with fear, which hinders my ability to receive and walk in Your love. I want to be free from fear. Forgive me, Lord, for opening this door for the enemy to come in to steal, kill and destroy. Today, I turn away from fear and turn toward You. Help me, Father God, to receive a greater revelation of Your love for me, that I will overflow with hope and leave no room for fear.

OTHER AREAS OF REPENTANCE

_____

_____

_____

DAY 2

Repent, then, and turn to God, so that your sins may be wiped out,
that times of refreshing may come from the Lord.
(Acts 3:19)

SUBMISSION

I am Your disciple, Father, and I want to be Your student so I can learn from You. I submit myself to You and Your ways of teaching me. I bring my fears to Your altar and ask that You would loose me from fear and enable Your love to be deeply rooted in my heart. Fill me with a greater revelation of Your love for me, that I could walk in perfect peace. In Jesus' Name.

OTHER AREAS OF SUBMISSION

Submit yourselves, then, to God.
(James 4:7)

FROM THE FATHER'S HEART

How I love you, Child of mine. You belong to Me and My love envelopes you daily. I lavish you with My love and pour out My love into

9

your heart by My Holy Spirit. As I pour out My love, pour it out onto others, that I may fill you more. As you grow in My love, fear cannot stand. You will walk in freedom and liberty as you come to full maturity.

PERSONAL WORD FROM MY FATHER

_____

_____

_____

_____

_____

_____

_____

_____

_____

_____

_____

_____

_____

_____

_____

_____

_____

_____

_____

_____

_____

Speak, LORD, for your servant is listening.
(1 Samuel 3:9)

DAY 3

Father, today I'm thankful for:

_____

_____

_____

_____

_____

_____

_____

_____

Meditation

Paul wrote to the Philippians, "I am certain that God, who began the good work within you, will continue his work until it is finally finished on the day when Christ Jesus returns" (Philippians 1:6 NLT). In spite of appearances and regardless of what some might think, God will complete the good work He started in me. God will continue His work in me until He brings it to completion. I must only believe.

May my meditation be pleasing to him, as I rejoice in the LORD.
(Psalm 104:34)

Scripture Focus

"Stop wailing," Jesus said. "She is not dead but asleep."
They laughed at him, knowing that she was dead.
(Luke 8:52b-53)

FOR REFLECTION

1. What promises has God given me, personally and through His Word, for which I've been standing?

_____

_____

_____

_____

_____

_____

2. Have any of God's promises appeared to have died an early death? Explain.

_____

_____

_____

_____

_____

_____

3. What have people told me about the promises God has given me? Who has encouraged me? Who has discouraged me?

_____

_____

_____

_____

_____

_____

4. My Father says, "Don't be afraid. Just believe." What does this statement mean to me?

_____

_____

_____

_____

_____

_____

Reflect on what I am saying, for the Lord will give you insight into all this.
(2 Timothy 2:7)

REPENTANCE

Merciful Father, I'm sorry for the times I've listened to and believed those who have wailed over the death of the promises and dreams You've given me. Forgive me for my lack of belief while I focused on appearances. Wash away my sin of unbelief, Lord, and help me become strong in faith.

OTHER AREAS OF REPENTANCE

_____

_____

_____

_____

_____

_____

Repent, then, and turn to God, so that your sins may be wiped out,
that times of refreshing may come from the Lord.
(Acts 3:19)

SUBMISSION

Most High God, I give You, again, all with which You have entrusted me. I thank You for the good work You've started in me and I trust that You will continue it until You complete that work. I will cooperate with You and Your plan, and will continue to believe Your promises in spite of my circumstances or appearances. In Jesus' Name.

OTHER AREAS OF SUBMISSION

_____

_____

_____

_____

_____

_____

Submit yourselves, then, to God.
(James 4:7)

FROM THE FATHER'S HEART

I rejoice in your renewed trust in Me! The dreams I have given you will surely come to pass. The good work I've started in you, I will bring to completion. Everything will happen according to My flawless plan and perfect timing. Be not afraid! Just believe. For you will see resurrection life in that which others have said is dead, and I shall be glorified in and through it.

DAY 3

PERSONAL WORD FROM MY FATHER

_____

_____

_____

_____

_____

_____

_____

_____

_____

_____

_____

_____

_____

_____

_____

_____

_____

_____

_____

_____

_____

_____

_____

Speak, LORD, for your servant is listening.
(1 Samuel 3:9)

DAY 4

Father, today I'm thankful for:

_____
_____
_____
_____
_____
_____
_____
_____
_____
_____

Meditation

My feelings, which are vulnerable and can change like the wind, do not determine my identity. God's Word, the unshakeable, immoveable, unchanging truth, determines who I am. In spite of how I feel, God's Word is the only truth on which I stand. When the accuser of the brethren brings his lies, I will prevail as I choose to stand on God's truth.

May my meditation be pleasing to him, as I rejoice in the LORD.
(Psalm 104:34)

Scripture Focus

*For the accuser of our brothers and sisters has been thrown down
to earth-the one who accuses them before our God day and night.
And they have defeated him by the blood of the Lamb and by their testimony.*
(Revelation 12:10-11, NLT)

FOR REFLECTION

1. With my heart open before God, what do I believe about my identity? I believe these things about myself:

_____

_____

_____

_____

_____

_____

2. In reviewing the above list, are my beliefs in agreement with what God says about me? Are my beliefs the truth or are they lies of the enemy?

_____

_____

_____

_____

_____

_____

3. Study and document five scriptures regarding my identity in Christ. Ask my Father to lead me to those scriptures that will address areas of weakness in me.

_____

_____

_____

_____

_____

_____

4. Verbalize the scriptures documented in question #3 daily. Write them on sticky notes and display them where I will see them regularly. Memorize them and speak them aloud daily.

_____

_____

_____

_____

_____

Reflect on what I am saying, for the Lord will give you insight into all this.
(2 Timothy 2:7)

REPENTANCE

O God, maker of heaven and earth, I come to You on bended knee. Forgive me, Lord God, for coming into agreement with the lies of the enemy and for wavering in my faith in You and Your Word. May Your Word be established in my life and my heart, directing me on the path of truth and righteousness.

OTHER AREAS OF REPENTANCE

_____

_____

_____

_____

Repent, then, and turn to God, so that your sins may be wiped out,
that times of refreshing may come from the Lord.
(Acts 3:19)

SUBMISSION

I surrender my mind to You, Lord. Your Word is truth, O God, and I desire for Your truth to light my path all of the days of my life. Make me aware of the snares of the enemy when he comes with lies that contradict Your Word. When his flaming arrows come, I will lift my shield of faith. In Jesus' Name.

OTHER AREAS OF SUBMISSION

_____

_____

_____

_____

_____

Submit yourselves, then, to God.
(James 4:7)

FROM THE FATHER'S HEART

My little lamb, I shall lead you always and will search for you when you go astray. You can trust Me to lead you to green pastures where you will find abundant life that I desire for you. My love for you is unfailing; I will never lead you on the wrong path. I am with you, even in the midst of the storm. After the storm, My Child, My rainbow comes. Without the storm, there can be no rainbow. Without the darkness of the night, the light of the day cannot arise. I am with you always, even to the end of the age.

PERSONAL WORD FROM MY FATHER

_____

_____

_____

_____

_____

_____

_____

_____

_____

_____

_____

_____

_____

_____

_____

_____

_____

_____

_____

_____

_____

_____

_____

_____

_____

Speak, LORD, for your servant is listening.
(1 Samuel 3:9)

DAY 5

Father, today I'm thankful for:

_____

_____

_____

_____

_____

_____

_____

_____

_____

_____

Meditation

It is my choice to trust God or to trust my circumstances. If I choose to trust Him, and put my confidence in Him, I can dwell in perfect peace. I cannot keep myself in perfect peace, only God can. But in order for Him to keep me in peace, I must do my part by trusting Him and His Word and putting my confidence in Him and His Word. I choose today to trust God.

May my meditation be pleasing to him, as I rejoice in the LORD.
(Psalm 104:34)

Scripture Focus

You will keep in perfect peace all who trust in you,
all whose thoughts are fixed on you!
(Isaiah 26:3, NLT)

FOR REFLECTION

1. What does "perfect peace" mean to me? How would I rate myself on the issue of peace?

_____

_____

_____

_____

_____

_____

2. *Peace* literally means "peace, safety, prosperity, well-being, wholeness and completeness." Recite Isaiah 26:3, inserting each of these words in place of the word *peace*.

_____

_____

_____

_____

_____

_____

3. What tangible ways can I grow and mature in the areas mentioned in #2?

_____

_____

_____

_____

_____

_____

4. Whose responsibility is it to keep me in perfect peace? Whose respon-
    sibility is it to trust God and put my confidence in Him? Are they
    dependent on each other?

_____

_____

_____

_____

_____

_____

Reflect on what I am saying, for the Lord will give you insight into all this.
(2 Timothy 2:7)

REPENTANCE

Dear God, how I have grieved You by my lack of trust in You. Forgive
me, O Lord, for I have sinned. I'm sorry for the ways in which I've forsaken
You and Your Word, instead choosing to put my trust in what I see or feel.
How I need your peace, Lord, and how I need Your help in growing to full
maturity in peace as I trust in You.

OTHER AREAS OF REPENTANCE

_____

_____

_____

_____

Repent, then, and turn to God, so that your sins may be wiped out,
that times of refreshing may come from the Lord.
(Acts 3:19)

SUBMISSION

Father, I know that Your ways are not my ways. You know what is best for me and You know the ways in which I learn best. I submit to Your training, Lord, and ask that You would help me to learn to trust You and put my confidence in You in a greater measure. In Jesus' Name.

OTHER AREAS OF SUBMISSION

_____

_____

_____

_____

_____

Submit yourselves, then, to God.
(James 4:7)

FROM THE FATHER'S HEART

Dear One, how I delight when you come before Me like a child. How I delight when you trust Me and take Me at My Word, following Me wherever I lead. I shall take you by the hand and lead you to a deeper place of trust. Come, follow Me. We will walk together all the days of your life.

D A Y   5

PERSONAL WORD FROM MY FATHER

Speak, LORD, for your servant is listening.
(1 Samuel 3:9)

DAY 6

Father, today I'm thankful for:

_____
_____
_____
_____
_____
_____
_____
_____
_____
_____

Meditation

God says that I can do all things through Him who strengthens me. Without Him, I can do nothing, I can change nothing, I can achieve nothing and I can overcome nothing. But through Him, and by His Spirit, I am an over comer! Daily, I will receive His strength and daily I will overcome.

May my meditation be pleasing to him, as I rejoice in the LORD.
(Psalm 104:34)

Scripture Focus

I tell you the truth, unless a kernel of wheat falls to the ground and dies, it remains only a single seed. But if it dies, it produces many seeds.
(John 12:24)

FOR REFLECTION

1. What areas of my life have yet to be surrendered to God?

2. Thinking of the areas mentioned above, how have I tried in my own strength to conquer them? Am I struggling in the flesh, or have I allowed God to work through me as an over comer? Have I worked by my might, by my power, or by God's Spirit?

3. In what areas of my life has God already enabled me to find victory? How did I overcome in those areas?

....

....

....

4. Am I prepared to surrender all to my Father, allowing Him to live through me and strengthen me by His Spirit? Document your thoughts.

....

....

....

....

....

....

Reflect on what I am saying, for the Lord will give you insight into all this.
(2 Timothy 2:7)

REPENTANCE

Heavenly Father, giver of life, forgive my futile efforts to overcome struggles in my own strength. I'm broken; I'm at the end of myself. I acknowledge the error of my ways, O God, and know I can do nothing without You, but can do everything through You. I desire to correct the error of my ways, Lord, and to walk fully in Your ways.

OTHER AREAS OF REPENTANCE

....

....

....

....

Repent, then, and turn to God, so that your sins may be wiped out,
that times of refreshing may come from the Lord.
(Acts 3:19)

SUBMISSION

Loving Father, I bring You my many failed attempts to change. I've tried to do things my way, but now surrender all to You and Your ways. I need Your help. May Your will, and not my will, be done, O God. I give You my body, soul and spirit, and ask that You make me more like You. I'm dependent on You for all, Lord God, and willingly give You my life. In Jesus' Name.

OTHER AREAS OF SUBMISSION

Submit yourselves, then, to God.
(James 4:7)

FROM THE FATHER'S HEART

Do not be afraid. For what you consider an ending is a beginning to Me, and in a beginning, I will do new things. Out of your brokenness, I will bring beauty. Out of death, I will bring life. Time is short and there is much for you to do. Do not be afraid, My child. For I, the Lord, am with you.

PERSONAL WORD FROM MY FATHER

Speak, LORD, for your servant is listening.
(1 Samuel 3:9)

DAY 7

Father, today I'm thankful for:

_____

_____

_____

_____

_____

_____

_____

_____

_____

_____

Meditation

Satan, the accuser, uses a hellacious megaphone to bring accusations against me. I will no longer allow him to have a voice of influence. When the enemy condemns me, my Father writes on my heart, "I Love You!" I am forgiven because I AM forgave me. Because of the shed blood of Jesus, my sin has been washed away and I stand before my Father white as snow. Because I am forgiven and free from the shame of my past, I can hold my head high, knowing I'm a child of the Most High God.

May my meditation be pleasing to him, as I rejoice in the LORD.
(Psalm 104:34)

Scripture Focus

"Then neither do I condemn you," Jesus declared. "Go now and leave your life of sin."
(John 8:11)

31

FOR REFLECTION

I. In what areas of my life can I relate to the woman caught in adultery? Does anything from my past cause me to feel shame or condemnation? Explain.

\
\
\
\
\
\

2. Have I ever sensed man's judgment toward me? If so, how has this judgment affected me?

\
\
\
\
\
\

3. Come before the Father with a humble heart. Tell Him about the situations where I felt judged or condemned and ask Him if He judges me. What was His response?

\
\
\
\

_____

_____

_____

4. Does anything from my past seem to haunt me on a regular basis? I will examine my heart for areas in need of repentance. Do I need to repent of unforgiveness toward those who have judged or condemned me? Forgiveness is available for me right now. I will confess my sin to my Father and be washed clean.

_____

_____

_____

_____

_____

_____

Reflect on what I am saying, for the Lord will give you insight into all this.
(2 Timothy 2:7)

REPENTANCE

Father of compassion, forgive me for allowing unconfessed sin to remain in my life. Forgive me for neglecting to receive Your gift of forgiveness. Though I hang my head in shame, I know You are the lifter of my head. Help me, O God, to respond to You when You put Your finger on areas I need to change. I come before You with a repentant heart today, and ask that You wash away my sin once again. As I leave my life of sin, help me to turn my life in a new direction.

OTHER AREAS OF REPENTANCE

_____

_____

_____

_____

_____

_____

Repent, then, and turn to God, so that your sins may be wiped out,
that times of refreshing may come from the Lord.
(Acts 3:19)

SUBMISSION

O God, though I have sinned against You, You have welcomed me into Your arms of grace and mercy, embracing me with your unfailing love. I'm grateful, Father, for Your patience with me as You awaited my return. I want to honor You in and through my life, Holy Lord, and I ask that You take me and make me what You created me to be in You. In Jesus' Name.

OTHER AREAS OF SUBMISSION

_____

_____

_____

_____

_____

_____

Submit yourselves, then, to God.
(James 4:7)

FROM THE FATHER'S HEART

I do not accuse you, My precious child. I embrace You today, and welcome You into My arms. I will never leave you or forsake you, even when you feel you have failed Me. I welcome you today with open arms, My love, and will always welcome you with open arms. I AM the God of love. I AM love and I will never change. You are mine and nobody can snatch you out of My mighty hand. You, little One, I have written on the palm of My righteous right hand.

PERSONAL WORD FROM MY FATHER

Speak, LORD, for your servant is listening.
(1 Samuel 3:9)

DAY 8

DATE: _____

Father, today I'm thankful for:

_____
_____
_____
_____
_____
_____
_____
_____
_____
_____

Meditation

My Father has a good plan for my life and has given me everything I need for life and godliness through my knowledge of Him who called me by His own glory and goodness. He provided me with His written Word as a roadmap to lead me and guide me through life. As I follow His plan, and stay within His established boundaries, He will cause me to prosper and live life to the fullest.

May my meditation be pleasing to him, as I rejoice in the LORD.
(Psalm 104:34)

Scripture Focus

This day I call heaven and earth as witnesses against you
that I have set before you life and death, blessings and curses.
Now choose life, so that you and your children may live.
(Deuteronomy 30:19)

FOR REFLECTION

1. What yellow caution lights has God put in my path to warn me to use extreme caution when I proceed? Have I heeded God's warnings? What was the result?

_____

_____

_____

_____

_____

_____

2. What stoplights has God put in my life? Did I stop and seek His direction or did I run the stoplight? What was the consequence of my choice?

_____

_____

_____

_____

_____

_____

3. As I reflect on the yellow and red lights God has put in my path, do I sense any guilt or condemnation for the times I may have disobeyed God's laws? Explain.

_____

_____

_____

_____
_____
_____
_____

4. Set some time aside to bask in God's presence. Turn my cell phone and computer off and talk to my Father about the experiences shared above. What have I learned?

_____
_____
_____
_____
_____
_____

Reflect on what I am saying, for the Lord will give you insight into all this.
(2 Timothy 2:7)

REPENTANCE

Lord of my life, here I am again with sin-stained hands asking Your forgiveness provided through Your blood-stained hands. I have knowingly strayed outside Your boundaries and chosen to go my own stubborn way. I've ignored the warning signals and stops You've put in my path. I'm sorry for my wrong attitude that surfaces when I suffer the consequences of my wrong choices. Help me, Lord, to become more like You.

OTHER AREAS OF REPENTANCE

_____
_____
_____

Repent, then, and turn to God, so that your sins may be wiped out,
that times of refreshing may come from the Lord.
(Acts 3:19)

SUBMISSION

God of all comfort, Father of compassion, here I am again, submitting myself to You. Thank You for welcoming me again, and for Your willingness to take my hand and lead me again, even when I've been unfaithful. I submit myself to Your plan, O God, and ask You to fill me with knowledge of Your will where my life is concerned. Give me eyes to recognize Your warnings and give me a heart of obedience to heed those warnings so You will be glorified through my life. In Jesus' Name.

OTHER AREAS OF SUBMISSION

Submit yourselves, then, to God.
(James 4:7)

FROM THE FATHER'S HEART

Come now, My child, and I will show you the way. For you are like a little child and must learn the boundaries I have established for your life.

Many dangers of which you are unaware lurk outside the boundaries, to steal, kill and destroy. I have come to bring you life and life abundantly! Trust Me and know that the warning signals and red lights I have put in your path are there for your good and for My glory.

PERSONAL WORD FROM MY FATHER

_____

_____

_____

_____

_____

_____

_____

_____

_____

_____

_____

_____

_____

_____

_____

_____

_____

_____

_____

_____

_____

Speak, LORD, for your servant is listening.
(I Samuel 3:9)

DAY 9

DATE: _____

Father, today I'm thankful for:

_____
_____
_____
_____
_____
_____
_____
_____
_____
_____

Meditation

My thoughts today will impact my actions tomorrow, and my actions today will impact my thoughts tomorrow. I can choose what I allow myself to meditate on and can choose to resist wrong thoughts, taking them captive and making them obedient to Christ.

May my meditation be pleasing to him, as I rejoice in the LORD.
(Psalm 104:34)

SCRIPTURE FOCUS

Whatever is true, whatever is noble, whatever is right,
whatever is pure, whatever is lovely, whatever is admirable—
if anything is excellent or praiseworthy—think about such things.
(Philippians 4:8)

FOR REFLECTION

1. As I evaluate my thought life, on what have my thoughts been focused? Have past emotional wounds consumed my thoughts? What thoughts do I need to take captive and make obedient to Christ?

---

2. Reflecting on the thoughts mentioned above, find several scriptures that I can use when destructive thoughts drop in unannounced.

---

3. Schedule a fast from wrong thoughts and trust my Father for the duration of the fast. When the enemy sends unwanted thoughts into my "inbox," choose to resist them, posting a sign that reads, *No Trespassing! God's Property!* Explain the results.

---

4. When I arise in the morning, consciously think about what is on my mind and choose to set my course with the right thoughts. What is this experience like for you?

Reflect on what I am saying, for the Lord will give you insight into all this.
(2 Timothy 2:7)

REPENTANCE

God and Father of my Lord Jesus, forgive me for allowing my mind to be the devil's playground. I'm sorry for the ways in which I've allowed wrong thoughts to dominate my mind, and for entertaining that which dishonors You. Forgive me, Lord, for sin that has resulted from an unrestrained thought life. Help me, O God, to purify my thought life and to post my *No Trespassing! God's Property!* sign when ungodly thoughts arrive unannounced.

OTHER AREAS OF REPENTANCE

_____

_____

_____

_____

Repent, then, and turn to God, so that your sins may be wiped out,
that times of refreshing may come from the Lord.
(Acts 3:19)

SUBMISSION

I give You my thought life today, Father God. Fill me with Your thoughts, fill me with Your ideas, fill my mind with that which will honor You. Make my mind a place where Your Spirit wants to dwell. Take hold of my thoughts as You take hold of my heart. Help me to recognize wrong thoughts and resist them instantly. In Jesus' Name.

Other areas of submission

_____

_____

_____

_____

_____

_____

Submit yourselves, then, to God.
(James 4:7)

FROM THE FATHER'S HEART

My cherished one, how I long to fill your body, soul and spirit with thoughts of Me. How I long for you to dwell in Me and My Word. As you hunger and thirst for Me, I shall fill you to overflowing. As You come near to Me, I come near to You. As you think on Me, I will release a sweet fragrance in your thoughts that will follow you wherever you go.

PERSONAL WORD FROM MY FATHER

Speak, LORD, for your servant is listening.
(1 Samuel 3:9)

DAY 10

Father, today I'm thankful for:

_____

_____

_____

_____

_____

_____

_____

_____

_____

Meditation

The devil has no authority over me. God has authority over the devil and has given me His authority to stand against him. When I submit myself to God and resist the devil, he must flee. I have no reason to fear the devil, as Jesus defeated him at the cross. As I remain in Christ, no weapon the devil forms against me can prosper.

May my meditation be pleasing to him, as I rejoice in the LORD.
(Psalm 104:34)

Scripture Focus

Be self-controlled and alert. Your enemy the devil prowls around like a roaring lion looking for someone to devour.
(I Peter 5:8)

FOR REFLECTION

1. As I ponder my journey with Jesus and the path I've walked with Him since the beginning, think of a time I may have strayed off the path into enemy territory. Explain.

2. What obstacles did I encounter when I ventured into unfamiliar territory?

3. Did I call on God for help? If not, why didn't I call on Him? How was I rescued and redirected onto the right path?

_____

_____

4. Am I afraid of the devil? Explain. Look up Luke 10:19, James 4:7 and
    Colossians 2:15 and meditate on these scriptures, write them below and
    memorize them.

_____

_____

_____

_____

_____

_____

Reflect on what I am saying, for the Lord will give you insight into all this.
(2 Timothy 2:7)

REPENTANCE

Loving Father, forgive me for the times I've strayed away from You and
ventured into enemy territory. I want to learn from the error of my ways,
Lord, so I might become better equipped for what is ahead. I'm sorry for
running in fear from the devil instead of standing in the authority You have
given me. O God, I need You.

OTHER AREAS OF REPENTANCE

_____

_____

_____

_____

Repent, then, and turn to God, so that your sins may be wiped out,
that times of refreshing may come from the Lord.
(Acts 3:19)

SUBMISSION

I come under the shadow of Your wing, Father. I desire to follow the path of righteousness You have set for me through Your Holy Word. Help me stay on the right path, O God, that I might not sin against You. Increase my understanding of the authority You have provided for me through the shed blood of Your Son, that I might walk in that authority wherever You send me. In Jesus' Name.

OTHER AREAS OF SUBMISSION

_____

_____

_____

_____

_____

_____

Submit yourselves, then, to God.
(James 4:7)

FROM THE FATHER'S HEART

My beloved, I am with you always, even when you stray off the path. Wherever you are, My precious one, turn to Me now. If you have wandered, turn back to Me where you are safe. My angels are round about you. I guard your path, My child, and protect your way. Do you not know that I look

after the lilies in the fields and the sparrows in the air? How much more do I care about and watch over you. Do not fear, for no one can snatch you out of My hand. You are sealed by My Spirit for all of eternity.

PERSONAL WORD FROM MY FATHER

Speak, LORD, for your servant is listening.
(1 Samuel 3:9)

DAY 11

Father, today I'm thankful for:

_____

_____

_____

_____

_____

_____

_____

_____

_____

_____

Meditation

I am pregnant with divine purpose! As the Holy Spirit has overshadowed me, I have conceived a spiritual pregnancy and with great delight I receive that which God is developing within me. He will walk me through the development, preparation and labor. This spiritual baby will be born for God's glory!

May my meditation be pleasing to him, as I rejoice in the LORD.
(Psalm 104:34)

Scripture Focus

The thief comes only to steal and kill and destroy;
I have come that they may have life, and have it to the full.
(John 10:10)

FOR REFLECTION

1. For what purpose do I believe God put me on the earth? Did I receive God's plan or have I distanced myself from it? Ponder the relation between physical pregnancy and spiritual pregnancy. Do I believe I am pregnant with purpose?

    _____

    _____

    _____

    _____

    _____

    _____

2. Has anyone told me that I would never accomplish what I believed God wanted me to do? Explain. What impact did this have on the way I viewed my calling?

    _____

    _____

    _____

    _____

    _____

    _____

3. Can I identify schemes of the devil to abort the plan for which God designed me? Explain.

    _____

    _____

_____

_____

_____

_____

_____

4. What stage of my spiritual pregnancy am I currently experiencing? Am I in the developmental stage or is it time for me to push through labor?

_____

_____

_____

_____

_____

_____

Reflect on what I am saying, for the Lord will give you insight into all this.
(2 Timothy 2:7)

REPENTANCE

Father God, Creator of heaven and earth, as I humble myself and examine my life, I recognize that I have failed in so many ways. Though You have equipped me with divine purpose, I have often doubted it would ever come to pass. I've listened to the lies of the enemy and believed I was unworthy to be used of You in such amazing ways. I'm sorry, Lord God, that as I've doubted myself, I've really been doubting You. I'm sorry, Father. Forgive me for my sin.

OTHER AREAS OF REPENTANCE

_____

_____

_____

_____

_____

_____

Repent, then, and turn to God, so that your sins may be wiped out,
that times of refreshing may come from the Lord.
(Acts 3:19)

SUBMISSION

O God, I leap and jump for joy at the news of my spiritual pregnancy! I embrace You now and I embrace what You are developing within me. I receive my callings with gratitude and submit myself to the path You have set before me in preparation for birth. I love You, Father, and though I don't know exactly what this spiritual baby will look like, I trust You to develop it according to Your perfect plan. I'm honored, Lord, to serve You. In Jesus' Name.

OTHER AREAS OF SUBMISSION

_____

_____

_____

_____

_____

_____

Submit yourselves, then, to God.
(James 4:7)

FROM THE FATHER'S HEART

Dearly beloved, you are My chosen vessel to birth My purpose. Do not despise the preparation and growth stages of what I am developing, as all

DAY 11

are necessary and critical. Embrace Me as you embrace My purpose. You will give birth at just the right time and all will marvel at what I have done in and through you. I'm a proud Daddy!

PERSONAL WORD FROM MY FATHER

_____

_____

_____

_____

_____

_____

_____

_____

_____

_____

_____

_____

_____

_____

_____

_____

_____

_____

_____

_____

_____

_____

_____

_____

_____

_____

_____

_____

_____

_____

Speak, LORD, for your servant is listening.
(1 Samuel 3:9)

DAY 12

DATE: _____

Father, today I'm thankful for:

_____

_____

_____

_____

_____

_____

_____

_____

_____

_____

_____

_____

Meditation

Jesus was always about His Father's business, doing only what the Father wanted Him to do. At times He even walked past people who were sick. Following His example, I will live a fruitful life if I ask for and receive direction from my Father before I commit to new activity.

May my meditation be pleasing to him, as I rejoice in the LORD.
(Psalm 104:34)

Scripture Focus

Be still before the LORD and wait patiently for him.
(Psalm 37:7)

FOR REFLECTION

1. Examine and document my current schedule of activities. Which activities are fruitful and which ones lack fruitfulness? Which activities bring me inner joy and which ones cause inner turmoil?

2. Reflecting on each activity listed in #1, did I pursue God's wisdom and direction before committing to this activity? Explain.

3. When needs arise, personally, spiritually and professionally, do I jump in to meet the need or do I prayerfully consider if it's something with which I should become involved? Do I know how to say "no"? Explain.

_____

_____

_____

_____

4. Set time aside to review my schedule with my Father and ask Him for divine guidance on possible adjustments to my commitments. When I receive His direction, prune what does not belong that I might become more fruitful.

_____

_____

_____

_____

_____

Reflect on what I am saying, for the Lord will give you insight into all this.
(2 Timothy 2:7)

REPENTANCE

Father of compassion, I've mucked up my life with so much activity that my time with You is often squeezed out. I'm sorry, O God! Fear of man has driven me into commitments I should not have made. Forgive me for caving in to the pressures and expectations of man instead of looking to You for direction. Help me, Lord God, I want to do what is pleasing in Your sight.

OTHER AREAS OF REPENTANCE

_____

_____

_____

DAY 12

Repent, then, and turn to God, so that your sins may be wiped out,
that times of refreshing may come from the Lord.
(Acts 3:19)

SUBMISSION

Lord God, I bring my schedule, my plans and my agenda to Your altar. I surrender all to You and invite You to help me prune my schedule. Cut out anything that is not part of Your divine plan. I give You permission to make necessary changes so I can be more fruitful for Your kingdom. In Jesus' Name.

OTHER AREAS OF SUBMISSION

Submit yourselves, then, to God.
(James 4:7)

FROM THE FATHER'S HEART

I have ordained your steps, treasured one, and have a wondrous plan for every season of your life. I delight when You come to Me for direction and marvel at the joy you experience when You fulfill the works for which I've created you. I hold the answers you need. I have the wisdom you need and

I have the keys you need to unlock the door of My divinely orchestrated plan. Ask and you will receive.

PERSONAL WORD FROM MY FATHER

_____
_____
_____
_____
_____
_____
_____
_____
_____
_____
_____
_____
_____
_____
_____
_____
_____
_____
_____
_____
_____
_____

Speak, LORD, for your servant is listening.
(1 Samuel 3:9)

DAY 13

Father, today I'm thankful for:

_____
_____
_____
_____
_____
_____
_____
_____
_____
_____
_____

Meditation

While Jesus hung on the cross with the sin of the world nailed through His hands and feet, He said, "My God, My God, why have You forsaken Me?" Jesus understands my feelings of abandonment and knows how it feels to be seemingly forgotten. But God hadn't forgotten Him, and He hasn't forgotten me! Though He seems far away, He is so close that He can feel the breath from my nostrils.

May my meditation be pleasing to him, as I rejoice in the LORD.
(Psalm 104:34)

Scripture Focus

But God remembered Noah and all the wild animals and the livestock that were with him in the ark, and he sent a wind over the earth, and the waters receded.
(Genesis 8:1)

FOR REFLECTION

1. Have I ever felt as if God had forgotten about me or didn't care about my suffering? Have I ever felt like an abandoned orphan? Explain.

    _____

    _____

    _____

    _____

    _____

2. At the time, how did I respond to feeling as if God had forgotten or abandoned me? Was I angry with Him? Did I feel rejected? Journal your thoughts.

    _____

    _____

    _____

    _____

    _____

3. Reflecting on previous seasons of apparent abandonment, how did God respond to me during that time? In looking back, where can I see His hand reaching into my loneliness?

    _____

    _____

    _____

_____
_____
_____
_____

4. Set some time aside to talk to my Father about the times I shared above. Tell Him how I felt as I walked through seasons when I felt abandoned, then listen. What is He saying to me?

_____
_____
_____
_____
_____

Reflect on what I am saying, for the Lord will give you insight into all this.
(2 Timothy 2:7)

REPENTANCE

My Lord and my Savior, I fall on my knees in repentance before You. You promised to never leave me or forsake me, yet at times I've believed a lie that You had forgotten me. I'm sorry, Father, for questioning Your presence in my life. I'm sorry, Father, for putting my faith in my feelings instead of in You. Cleanse me, God, wash me clean again, O God.

OTHER AREAS OF REPENTANCE

_____
_____
_____
_____

_____

_____

_____

Repent, then, and turn to God, so that your sins may be wiped out,
that times of refreshing may come from the Lord.
(Acts 3:19)

SUBMISSION

Father God, Lord of my life, I bow my heart before You and surrender every circumstance of my life to You. Teach me, God, to be ever aware of Your presence, even when it feels like You're not there. Even if everyone else abandons me, I know You will never abandon me. With heart lifted high, I shall walk with You. I shall talk with You and I shall remain one with You all the days of my life. In Jesus' Name.

OTHER AREAS OF SUBMISSION

_____

_____

_____

_____

_____

_____

Submit yourselves, then, to God.
(James 4:7)

FROM THE FATHER'S HEART

When everyone seems to have forgotten you, I remember you. When your enemies rise up against you, I remember you. When you feel alone and discouraged, I remember you. Even when you are in sin, I remember you.

When the walls seem to be closing in on you and it seems as if you will never emerge from the wilderness, I remember you. My child, you are always on My mind. I have never missed even one second of your life. I will never, ever leave you or forsake you.

PERSONAL WORD FROM MY FATHER

Speak, LORD, for your servant is listening.
(1 Samuel 3:9)

DAY 14

Father, today I'm thankful for:

_____

_____

_____

_____

_____

_____

_____

_____

_____

_____

Meditation

I have no need to hide anything about myself from my loving Father. He already knows every detail about me and loves me right where I am, character flaws and all. Instead of denying my dire need for change, I will acknowledge the truth of who I am and submit myself to God so He can give me a new name. I will stay in the ring and wrestle with God until His purpose is fulfilled in me.

May my meditation be pleasing to him, as I rejoice in the LORD
(Psalm 104:34)

Scripture Focus

"What is your name?" the man asked. He replied, "Jacob."
(Genesis 32:27, NLT)

FOR REFLECTION

1. Humble myself before the Lord and acknowledge my character strengths and character flaws. List them now.

2. What areas of my character have I wanted to change but not yet found success? What has hindered me from changing?

3. What adjustments will become necessary if I allow God to change my character flaws? Will my environment need to change? Will the people with whom I surround myself need to change?

_____

_____

_____

4. Set some time aside to get quiet before God. "What is your name?" He
    asks. Tell my Father about myself, who I am and what I want to change.
    If led, get in the ring with God for a wrestling match and don't let go
    until He changes me.

_____

_____

_____

_____

_____

Reflect on what I am saying, for the Lord will give you insight into all this.
(2 Timothy 2:7)

REPENTANCE

Holy and righteous God, You are perfect, without flaw, yet I am imper-
fect and flawed in so many ways. I've strived to change myself in my own
strength and have found no success. I have failed to renew my mind with
Your Word to bring transformation to my life. Give me a greater hunger for
You, Your Word and Your righteousness, God. I'm holding on to You and
won't let go until You bless me.

OTHER AREAS OF REPENTANCE

_____

_____

_____

_____

_____

_____

_____

Repent, then, and turn to God, so that your sins may be wiped out,
that times of refreshing may come from the Lord.
(Acts 3:19)

SUBMISSION

Father, I want a new name. I willingly enter a wrestling match with You and want You to take me to the mat. Pin me to the floor, God. Do whatever You need to do in me so that I might be changed into the image of Your Son, Jesus. Transform my character to reflect your beauty. Here I am, O Lord, do whatever You need to do to change me into the person You created me to be. In Jesus' Name.

OTHER AREAS OF SUBMISSION

_____

_____

_____

_____

_____

_____

Submit yourselves, then, to God.
(James 4:7)

FROM THE FATHER'S HEART

Child of Mine, I named you while you were being formed in your mother's womb. I knew you from the beginning and delight in watching you grow. I called you by name and appointed you to lift My Name in the earth. Submit yourself to Me daily, surrender all to Me. As we walk together, I will change you, prune you, and love you into the person I created you to be in Me. Just walk with Me. Just *be* in Me. I will change you from the inside out and even you will marvel at the work of My hand.

PERSONAL WORD FROM MY FATHER

Speak, LORD, for your servant is listening.
(1 Samuel 3:9)

DAY 15

Father, today I'm thankful for:

_____
_____
_____
_____
_____
_____
_____
_____
_____
_____
_____

Meditation

God's goodness leads me to repent. When the conviction of the Holy Spirit helps me recognize my sin, I can respond in repentance so He can lead me in a new direction. Condemnation is from the enemy, not from God. As I acknowledge my sin before God, He will strengthen me to do an about face and will lead me by the hand in a new direction that leads to His abundant life.

May my meditation be pleasing to him, as I rejoice in the LORD.
(Psalm 104:34)

Scripture Focus

*If my people, who are called by my name, will humble themselves
and pray and seek my face and turn from their wicked ways, then will
I hear from heaven and will forgive their sin and will heal their land.*
(2 Chronicles: 7:14)

FOR REFLECTION

1. In what areas of my life has God been bringing conviction of sin?

2. How have I responded to the conviction of the Holy Spirit? Have I listened and followed God's direction or have I ignored it?

3. God's goodness leads to repentance. What does this statement mean to me?

_____

_____

4. Reflect on the items listed in #1 above. Am I ready to do an About Face to turn from my sin, and start in the right direction? What scriptures can I stand on and use to renew my mind as I start in a new direction?

_____

_____

_____

_____

_____

_____

Reflect on what I am saying, for the Lord will give you insight into all this.
(2 Timothy 2:7)

REPENTANCE

Amazing Lord of life, I cry out to You for mercy. My life has been plagued with unrighteous living, ungodly thoughts and selfish actions. I need a new direction that only You can provide. I've failed in so many says, Father, and I ask Your forgiveness as I've fallen short in Your sight. I see my sin and I want to do an About Face. I turn from my sin and turn toward You, God. Cleanse me of my wickedness and put me on Your path of righteousness.

OTHER AREAS OF REPENTANCE

_____

_____

_____

_____

Repent, then, and turn to God, so that your sins may be wiped out,
that times of refreshing may come from the Lord.
(Acts 3:19)

SUBMISSION

My God, my God! I have enlisted in Your Army and submit myself to Your authority. I will listen and respond to Your call, and will follow the path You have set before me. May sin be far from me as You cloak me in Your righteousness. I want Your will to be done in my life, O Most High God. I welcome Your help daily as I turn from the temptation of sin and fall into Your loving arms that will embrace me always. In Jesus' Name.

OTHER AREAS OF SUBMISSION

_____

_____

_____

_____

_____

_____

Submit yourselves, then, to God.
(James 4:7)

FROM THE FATHER'S HEART

I am here always for you, My beloved one. I remove your sin stained clothes and clothe you in My glory and My righteousness. As I put my finger on areas of sinfulness, respond to My leading. Leave sin behind, turn from it quickly, and you will see My glory shine. The temptation of the evil

one appears to entice you into sin, but it leads to death. My path of righteousness leads to life everlasting. Come. Follow Me to life everlasting.

PERSONAL WORD FROM MY FATHER

Speak, LORD, for your servant is listening.
(I Samuel 3:9)

DAY 16

Father, today I'm thankful for:

_____

_____

_____

_____

_____

_____

_____

_____

_____

_____

_____

Meditation

Compassion is part of God's nature and therefore, is part of my nature. Though I am moved with compassion toward others, I must stay in tune to the leading of the Holy Spirit in order to respond in line with God's plan. If He leads me to step in to help, I must obey. And if He leads me to step back, I must step back. If I step in when I'm supposed to step back, I can interfere with what God is doing in another's life. God sees the big picture; I only see a tiny piece of the picture.

May my meditation be pleasing to him, as I rejoice in the LORD.
(Psalm 104:34)

Scripture Focus

The LORD is good and does what is right; he shows the proper path to those who go astray.
(Psalm 25:8, NLT)

FOR REFLECTION

1. Think back to a time I was moved with compassion toward someone in need. Recount the story.

_____

_____

_____

_____

_____

_____

_____

2. Did I feel led to take action on this person's behalf? What did I do? As I examine my motives, what motivated me to help him or her?

_____

_____

_____

_____

_____

_____

3. What was the result of my actions? What did I learn from this situation?

_____

_____

_____

_____

_____

_____

4. Ask God to teach me about the subject of compassion as I search the gospels for times when Jesus was moved with compassion. What did I learn from Jesus?

_____

_____

_____

_____

_____

_____

Reflect on what I am saying, for the Lord will give you insight into all this.
(2 Timothy 2:7)

REPENTANCE

Holy Lord, forgive me for thinking I knew best how to help others in need. Forgive me for the times I've stepped into other people's lives when I should have stepped back. Forgive me for the times I haven't asked You for direction, then jumped in prematurely to rescue those I thought were drowning in life's circumstances. As I look back, I see that I may have interfered with Your plan by trying to rescue others from suffering. I'm sorry, O God, for trying to be a savior to others instead of pointing them to You, the one and only Savior of the world.

OTHER AREAS OF REPENTANCE

_____

_____

_____

_____

Repent, then, and turn to God, so that your sins may be wiped out,
that times of refreshing may come from the Lord.
(Acts 3:19)

SUBMISSION

Father of compassion, God of all comfort, here I am, Lord. I am available to You today. Use me as a tool to demonstrate Your compassion to others. Keep me, O Lord, from deception and protect me from those who might want to misuse or take advantage of my compassion. Please open my spiritual eyes and ears to see and hear the leading of Your Spirit. Activate the spirit of discernment so I will know when to step in to help and when to step back. Help me grow in compassion, while always pointing others to You, the one true God. In Jesus' Name.

OTHER AREAS OF SUBMISSION

_____

_____

_____

_____

_____

_____

Submit yourselves, then, to God.
(James 4:7)

FROM THE FATHER'S HEART

My little lamb, follow Me. Listen to My voice. You know My voice and can hear My voice through the many avenues through which I speak. You don't need to understand everything, nor do you need to figure out the details of My instruction. Just listen and obey as I show you the way. I am the Good Shepherd and will always lead you according to My will. My will is built on love and is flawless in every way.

PERSONAL WORD FROM MY FATHER

Speak, LORD, for your servant is listening.
(1 Samuel 3:9)

DAY 17

Father, today I'm thankful for:

_____

_____

_____

_____

_____

_____

_____

_____

_____

_____

Meditation

I am in the world, but not of this world. While on this earth, I have the privilege of choosing what I see, hear and speak. The input I allow through these avenues will impact the output that comes through my life. That with which I fill my heart will be evidenced in what comes from my mouth. I am a living epistle for all people to read.

May my meditation be pleasing to him, as I rejoice in the LORD.
(Psalm 104:34)

Scripture Focus

For it is written: "Be holy, because I am holy."
(1 Peter 1:16)

FOR REFLECTION

1. With a humble heart, examine my mouth. Have the words of my mouth built others up and honored God or have they been destructive and dishonorable? Explain.

_____

_____

_____

_____

_____

_____

2. With a humble heart, examine what I've allowed myself to watch or see. Have I guarded what I allow my eyes to gaze upon or has my conscience been seared?

_____

_____

_____

_____

_____

3. With a humble heart, examine what I've allowed myself to hear. Do I listen to inappropriate talk, gossip and slander? What standards have I set for movies and television? Have I loosened my standards?

_____

_____

_____

DAY 17

_____

_____

_____

4. In view of the preceding questions, what steps can I take to hear no evil, speak no evil and see no evil?

_____

_____

_____

_____

_____

_____

Reflect on what I am saying, for the Lord will give you insight into all this.
(2 Timothy 2:7)

REPENTANCE

Lord God, as I examine my heart, I come before You with a humbled heart of repentance. I have spoken, listened to and looked at things of this world that are dishonorable to You and that grieve Your Spirit. Cleanse me of my sin, Father, through the shed blood of Jesus. Forgive me, dear God, for knowingly and unknowingly entertaining sin through the world's means of entertainment. Help me, Lord Jesus, to guard my heart, my eyes, my ears and my mouth. Strengthen me and give me wisdom to lift up a standard in me that will represent You honorably.

OTHER AREAS OF REPENTANCE

_____

_____

_____

_____

_____

_____

_____

Repent, then, and turn to God, so that your sins may be wiped out,
that times of refreshing may come from the Lord.
(Acts 3:19)

SUBMISSION

Take my mouth, Lord, and help me speak words that align with Your Word to build and encourage others. Take my ears, Lord, and help me listen to words that bring life. Take my eyes, Lord, and help me look upon what is pure and lovely. Put guards around my mouth, my ears and my eyes, that I might honor You. In Jesus' Name.

Other areas of submission

_____

_____

_____

_____

_____

_____

_____

Submit yourselves, then, to God.
(James 4:7)

FROM THE FATHER'S HEART

I have put you in this world, but you are not of this world. I have chosen you as My representative on the earth. Though much evil surrounds you, I shall enable and strengthen you to remain pure in My sight. But you must have My ways foremost in your heart and resist the ways of the world. You must have My Word written on the tablet of your heart and you must walk close with Me. Together, we will radiate My glory for all to see.

PERSONAL WORD FROM MY FATHER

Speak, LORD, for your servant is listening.
(I Samuel 3:9)

DAY 18

Father, today I'm thankful for:

_____

_____

_____

_____

_____

_____

_____

_____

_____

_____

Meditation

God has a perfect plan for my life and has provided everything I need to accomplish that plan. If I seek and follow my loving Father's plan, I will find peace as I walk out His divinely orchestrated plan. If my priorities are His priorities, I will find perfect peace, plentiful provision and sufficient strength. If I lack peace, provision and strength, He will show me areas needing adjustment, if I am willing to listen and obey.

May my meditation be pleasing to him, as I rejoice in the LORD.
(Psalm 104:34)

Scripture Focus

I know, O LORD, that a man's life is not his own;
it is not for man to direct his steps.
(Jeremiah 10:23)

FOR REFLECTION

1. What are my top five priorities? List them. How much of my available time is assigned to each priority listed? How do I feel about where I'm spending the majority of my time?

    _____

    _____

    _____

    _____

    _____

2. Did I create my priority list or did man create it for me? Was God involved in establishing my activities? Explain.

    _____

    _____

    _____

    _____

    _____

3. Where does God fit in my priority list? Have I made time for prayer and study of His Word? Have I given myself permission to allow times of rest when I have no obligations, no distractions and no work? If not, do I need to schedule some downtime?

    _____

    _____

    _____

_____

_____

4. What priorities are causing me personal conflict? What priorities are causing conflict within my family? Pay particular attention to those activities that cause me to strive and sweat to get the job done. Talk to God about the conflicts, ask Him if I need to re prioritize and document what He shows me.

_____

_____

_____

_____

Reflect on what I am saying, for the Lord will give you insight into all this.
(2 Timothy 2:7)

REPENTANCE

Lord Jesus, I have been running in circles, striving and sweating to accomplish many things that may not have been ordained by You. I'm out of control. Father, I don't want to invest any more precious time in something that will burn up as wood, hay or stubble. Although I have claimed that You were my top priority, my actions have indicated otherwise. Dear God, forgive me. I'm sorry, Father, for taking our relationship for granted. Forgive me for striving and sweating to get jobs done when I'm not sure you've assigned the jobs to me in the first place. Have mercy on me, God, a sinner.

OTHER AREAS OF REPENTANCE

_____

_____

_____

Repent, then, and turn to God, so that your sins may be wiped out,
that times of refreshing may come from the Lord.
(Acts 3:19)

SUBMISSION

Most High God, precious Savior, I offer You my life today. I offer You my flawed priority list and ask You to transform my priority list into Your priority list. I want only what You want. Take away any wood, hay or stubble and replace it with purpose filled action. Father, align my will with Your will. Align my schedule with Your schedule. I don't want to run in circles any longer, Father. May Your peace, Your provision and Your strength lead me on a steady course as You guide me on Your perfectly paved path of purpose. In Jesus' Name.

OTHER AREAS OF SUBMISSION

Submit yourselves, then, to God.
(James 4:7)

FROM THE FATHER'S HEART

Do you know, Child, that I delight in you? Do you know how proud I am of you? I smile on you today, and welcome you as you come to Me for guidance. I've watched you run in circles trying to please Me. But you need not run, you need not strive. My plan is a perfect plan of peace and as you set your course to honor Me and My plan, My perfect peace will always go before you. When you don't sense My peace, stop. If My peace is not present, I say, "Do not move." Follow My peace and you will find great joy in serving Me. My peace I give you today, My beloved.

PERSONAL WORD FROM MY FATHER

Speak, LORD, for your servant is listening.
(1 Samuel 3:9)

DAY 19

Father, today I'm thankful for:

_____

_____

_____

_____

_____

_____

_____

_____

_____

_____

Meditation

Because God is a just God, a price had to be paid for the punishment of my sin. Although I deserved eternal separation from God, sickness and disease, my Father loved me so much that He sent Jesus, His only begotten Son to pay the penalty for my sin. The Lamb of God offers a love-laced package deal, given freely to all who will receive. Every drop of shed blood said, "You are forgiven." Every stripe on His back said, "You are healed." I receive. In Jesus' Name, I receive.

May my meditation be pleasing to him, as I rejoice in the LORD.
(Psalm 104:34)

Scripture Focus

Christ redeemed us from the curse of the law by becoming a curse for us,
for it is written: "Cursed is everyone who is hung on a tree."
(Galatians 3:13)

FOR REFLECTION

1. What has been my belief about God's ability to heal physical sickness and disease? On what have those beliefs been based?

_____

_____

_____

_____

_____

_____

2. Is Jesus Christ my Lord and Savior? Explain the difference between "Lord" and "Savior."

_____

_____

_____

_____

_____

_____

3. What package deal did Jesus offer the paralyzed man in Luke 5? Jesus told the paralytic that he was forgiven, then told him he could pick up his mat and go home. What is the relation between these two statements?

_____

_____

_____

_____

_____

_____

4. Read Deuteronomy 28, then read Galatians 3:10-13. Are there any sick-
    nesses or diseases not covered in the curse of the Law in Deuteronomy
    28? What does, "Christ redeemed us from the curse of the law by
    becoming a curse for us" mean to me?

_____

_____

_____

_____

Reflect on what I am saying, for the Lord will give you insight into all this.
(2 Timothy 2:7)

REPENTANCE

Lord God, I kneel before You and plead for mercy and grace. It is only by
Your grace that I have not perished for my lack of knowledge. Jesus, Your
demonstration of love awes me and paves the way for my forgiveness. I repent
of my unbelief, Father. I repent of my lack of knowledge of Your Word. I
didn't realize the great price that was paid so that I could not only be forgiven
of sin, but that I might walk in complete wholeness and health. I'm sorry,
Father, for willingly accepting flawed teachings without digging into Your
Word for the truth. Today, I accept Jesus as my Savior, and as my Healer.

OTHER AREAS OF REPENTANCE

_____

_____

_____

_Repent, then, and turn to God, so that your sins may be wiped out,
that times of refreshing may come from the Lord._
(Acts 3:19)

SUBMISSION

Jesus, Your Word says that You sent Your Word and healed us. I receive that living Word today. I receive You as Healer. Write Your truths on the tablet of my heart that it might illuminate my path and light the way for others. Expand my understanding of Your Word where healing is concerned. Use my hands to lay hands on the sick. Release Your healing anointing in me and make me a demonstration of Your healing power. Thank You, Father, that by the stripes of Your Son Jesus, I am healed. In Jesus' Name.

OTHER AREAS OF SUBMISSION

Submit yourselves, then, to God.
(James 4:7)

FROM THE FATHER'S HEART

I AM the Great Physician. I AM your Lord. I AM your Savior. I AM your Healer. I have made provision for everything you need, body, soul and

DAY 19

spirit. As you grow in knowledge of Me and My Word, you will walk in a greater understanding and a greater demonstration of My power. My people perish for their lack of understanding. My people perish, for they don't know Me. But you shall know Me. When you seek Me, you will find Me, when you seek Me with all of your heart.

PERSONAL WORD FROM MY FATHER

_____

_____

_____

_____

_____

_____

_____

_____

_____

_____

_____

_____

_____

_____

_____

_____

_____

_____

_____

_____

_____

Speak, LORD, for your servant is listening.
(1 Samuel 3:9)

DAY 20

Father, today I'm thankful for:

_____

_____

_____

_____

_____

_____

_____

_____

_____

_____

Meditation

God guards my path and protects my way. He laid out the entire plan for my life before even one day came to pass. He knows my past, He knows my today and He knows my future. I can trust Him with my life, knowing that He has a good plan He designed for my good and for His glory. If I trust Him with all my heart and do not lean on my own understanding, He will guard my heart and my mind in Christ Jesus.

May my meditation be pleasing to him, as I rejoice in the LORD.
(Psalm 104:34)

Scripture Focus

So let's not get tired of doing what is good.
At just the right time we will reap a harvest of blessing if we don't give up.
(Galatians 6:9, NLT)

FOR REFLECTION

1. What do I believe is the ideal way to discern the "right" time and the "wrong" time? How can I identify each?

    _____

    _____

    _____

    _____

    _____

    _____

2. Give an example of a time in which I acted at the "right" time and an example of a time in which I acted at the "wrong" time. What were the results of both situations?

    _____

    _____

    _____

    _____

    _____

    _____

3. Has frustration or weariness ever caused me to push a door open before God's ideal time? What happened? What did I learn from the experience?

    _____

    _____

    _____

_____

_____

_____

4. Am I tired of waiting for something specific to come to pass? Explain. Do
    I need to release this situation to God and surrender my plan to His plan?

....

....

....

....

....

....

Reflect on what I am saying, for the Lord will give you insight into all this.
(2 Timothy 2:7)

REPENTANCE

Lord God, I am guilty of demanding my own way once again, instead
of trusting You to bring the details of my life together in Your timing. I've
failed to trust You countless times and often forget that Your plan is a
perfect plan that You brought to life through Your unfailing love for me.
Please forgive me, Father, and teach me to learn from the error of my ways.

OTHER AREAS OF REPENTANCE

....

....

....

....

....

Repent, then, and turn to God, so that your sins may be wiped out,
that times of refreshing may come from the Lord.
(Acts 3:19)

SUBMISSION

God, I bring my expectations and dreams to Your altar and offer them as a sacrifice unto You. I don't want anything You have planned for my life to come to pass before its time. I don't want to birth anything prematurely, yet I don't want to be overdue. I want to be right on time according to Your will. I surrender, Lord, all that I am and all that I want to do, to You. I surrender my family and my loved ones to You. I surrender my work, my ministry and my goals to You. I surrender all. Have Your way in me. In Jesus' Name.

OTHER AREAS OF SUBMISSION

Submit yourselves, then, to God.
(James 4:7)

FROM THE FATHER'S HEART

I understand your frustration and I understand your weariness as you wait for My perfect plan to come to pass. My plan is a perfect one, and it will come to pass just as I planned. I know the beginning from the end. I am already in your tomorrow, with a wondrous plan for you. If only you knew what I have in store for you! It will be well worth the wait, my little one. If you trust Me and rest in Me, you will see that all will be well!

PERSONAL WORD FROM MY FATHER

_____

_____

_____

_____

_____

_____

_____

_____

_____

_____

_____

_____

_____

_____

_____

_____

_____

_____

_____

_____

_____

_____

Speak, LORD, for your servant is listening.
(1 Samuel 3:9)

DAY 21

Father, today I'm thankful for:

_____

_____

_____

_____

_____

_____

_____

_____

_____

_____

Meditation

My ways are not God's ways and my thoughts are not His thoughts. Though much has happened that I do not understand, and many questions remain unanswered, I can choose to trust my heavenly Father, who loves me. My God is a God of love. He *IS* love, and always acts in love. Though I don't always understand the details of my circumstances, I choose to trust in the Lord with all of my heart.

May my meditation be pleasing to him, as I rejoice in the LORD.
(Psalm 104:34)

Scripture Focus

"For my thoughts are not your thoughts,
neither are your ways my ways," declares the LORD.
(Isaiah 55:8)

FOR REFLECTION

1. Have I ever lost a loved one whose death made no sense to me? Have I suffered another loss that I didn't understand? Explain.

    _____

    _____

    _____

    _____

    _____

    _____

2. How did I respond to the described situations? What was my response to God? What was my response to others? Did this situation drive me closer to God or further away from Him?

    _____

    _____

    _____

    _____

    _____

    _____

3. What questions did I want to ask God about this loss? In reviewing my list of questions, which questions has God answered? Which questions are still unanswered?

    _____

    _____

    _____

---

4. When I am ready, I can bring my unanswered questions to God. Am I willing to release my unresolved issue to God in spite of not having answers? I can tell my Father what I feel about my losses and then be still and listen for His voice. What is He speaking to me today?

Reflect on what I am saying, for the Lord will give you insight into all this.
(2 Timothy 2:7)

REPENTANCE

God of love, I see the error of my ways. I've often questioned You when I haven't understood the circumstances of life. I've blamed You for taking what is precious to me and I've accused You of not caring about me and my loved ones. Glorious Father, forgive me of my great sinfulness. You are faithful! Your ways are perfect. Create in me a new heart, O God, that trusts You completely in spite of what circumstances I may face.

OTHER AREAS OF REPENTANCE

_____

_____

_____

Repent, then, and turn to God, so that your sins may be wiped out,
That times of refreshing may come from the Lord.
(Acts 3:19)

SUBMISSION

Father God, Lord of the universe, I've been troubled by unanswered questions. Today, I give You my questions. I will trust You in spite of unanswered questions. I've wavered in my faith because I haven't understood situations that You've allowed. Today, I give you my lack of understanding. I will trust You in spite of my lack of understanding. I put my trust in You, and will go forth with confidence knowing that every detail of my life is in Your faithful hands. In Jesus' Name.

OTHER AREAS OF SUBMISSION

_____

_____

_____

_____

_____

_____

Submit yourselves, then, to God.
(James 4:7)

FROM THE FATHER'S HEART

I surround you with My favor as with a shield, My precious one. You can walk daily with confidence in Me, knowing that all I allow is part of My divine plan. It pleases Me when you trust Me when nothing makes sense. It delights Me when you rejoice in Me, even when your surroundings seem to contradict what you believe is right. I am good, always. I love you, always. And My plan is a perfect plan, always. As you trust Me with that which you do not understand, you will see My glorious plan unfold, all for your good and for My glory!

PERSONAL WORD FROM MY FATHER

Speak, LORD, for your servant is listening.
(1 Samuel 3:9)

DAY 22

Father, today I'm thankful for:

_____

_____

_____

_____

_____

_____

_____

_____

_____

Meditation

As I live to please God, I can live in complete peace. I have no fear of man or what man can do to me. Man's opinion of me is irrelevant. I live for the pleasure of my loving Father, who watches over me every moment. My desire is to enter His glory to hear, "Well done, my good and faithful servant!" I will not forget who I am in Christ, I will not forget that I'm about my Father's business and I won't forget that I represent Christ in the earth. I may be the only Jesus some will ever see.

May my meditation be pleasing to him, as I rejoice in the LORD.
(Psalm 104:34)

Scripture Focus

Let love and faithfulness never leave you; bind them around your neck, write them on the tablet of your heart. Then you will win favor and a good name in the sight of God and man.
(Proverbs 3:3-4)

FOR REFLECTION

1. How do I feel about the ways in which I've represented Jesus? Identify my strengths and my weaknesses.

2. Consider some of the primary activities in which I am involved as I humble myself before the Lord. What is my motivation for succeeding in these endeavors?

3. In what ways have I feared man's opinion of me? How have I responded when I didn't receive man's approval? Have I ever had to stand alone, obeying what God has asked of me in spite of not having man's approval? Explain.

_____

_____

_____

_____

_____

4. In what ways have I been a poor representative of Jesus on the earth? As I take time to reflect on this question, do I need to repent before God or man for representing Christ dishonorably?

_____

_____

_____

_____

_____

Reflect on what I am saying, for the Lord will give you insight into all this.
(2 Timothy 2:7)

REPENTANCE

I bow before You with a heavy heart, my God. I've sought after man's approval, Lord Jesus. Fear of man has hindered my obedience to You. I've tried to justify my reputation when others have falsely accused me or judged me for my past behaviors. Forgive me, God! Forgive me for my poor judgment. Deliver me from fear of man, that I might live only to please You.

OTHER AREAS OF REPENTANCE

_____

_____

_____

Repent, then, and turn to God, so that your sins may be wiped out,
that times of refreshing may come from the Lord.
(Acts 3:19)

SUBMISSION

Father God, I seek Your face today. I want to serve You and You alone. I want Your approval and Your approval alone. You are my God, and I submit myself to You and You alone. Capture my heart as you captured the Apostle Paul's heart. Change me on my road to Damascus, take the scales from my eyes! Fuel my heart with the fire of the Holy Spirit as I seek You with all of my heart. In Jesus' Name.

OTHER AREAS OF SUBMISSION

Submit yourselves, then, to God.
(James 4:7)

FROM THE FATHER'S HEART

My Holy Spirit dwells within you, as We have made Our home in you through My Son. You are the temple of the Holy Spirit, the Spirit of the

Living God. You are *in Me.* You are *about Me* and you *represent Me.* Your reputation before man matters not. Follow Me and follow My ways, even if you are of no reputation with man. Because I AM your advocate, you have nothing to fear. Fear of man will prove to be a snare. Fear Me alone.

PERSONAL WORD FROM MY FATHER

Speak, LORD, for your servant is listening.
(1 Samuel 3:9)

DAY 23

Father, today I'm thankful for:

_____

_____

_____

_____

_____

_____

_____

_____

_____

_____

Meditation

God's Word is truth. It has been forever settled in heaven and will never change. When all else passes away, the solid foundation of His Word will stand. I can trust His promises regardless of what circumstances surround me today. I am not moved by what I see, I am moved by faith. My Father is moved by childlike faith and will move in my environment today, even if my circumstances appear hopeless.

May my meditation be pleasing to him, as I rejoice in the LORD.
(Psalm 104:34)

Scripture Focus

I tell you the truth, anyone who will not receive the kingdom of God like a little child will never enter it.
(Mark 10:15)

FOR REFLECTION

1. Think of a time I witnessed childlike faith in action in my life or in someone else's life. Describe what I witnessed.

_____

_____

_____

_____

_____

_____

2. What does "childlike faith" mean to me? Why do I believe my Father wants me to have childlike faith?

_____

_____

_____

_____

_____

_____

3. What am I facing today that challenges my faith? Explain. What do I need from God today?

_____

_____

_____

_____

4. In relation to question #3, what Biblical promises can I profess as I stand in faith? Record these scriptures and speak them out loud daily. Can I say, "God's Word says it...I believe it...That settles it!"? Can I receive God's promises with childlike faith without trying to figure out the details?

Reflect on what I am saying, for the Lord will give you insight into all this.
(2 Timothy 2:7)

REPENTANCE

Everlasting Father, my lack of faith has caused lack in many areas of my life. As I've tried to figure You out, my intellect has gotten in the way of childlike faith. I've put You in a box, unknowingly limiting the areas of which I believed You would want to be involved. In repentance, I demolish those boundaries today and give You access to every part of my life. I open my heart and ask You to cleanse me of my sin of unbelief. I want to be childlike again, Father.

OTHER AREAS OF REPENTANCE

....

....

....

....

Repent, then, and turn to God, so that your sins may be wiped out,
that times of refreshing may come from the Lord.
(Acts 3:19)

SUBMISSION

O Father, how I love You! I run into Your open arms once again and embrace You as my loving Daddy. Your love astounds me and the mercy You've shown me, even in my spiritual tantrums, leaves me in awe. I'm grateful that You continue to love me right where I am, and that You respond to me, in spite of my failures and lack of faith. Teach me, Daddy, to walk daily in childlike faith that I might please You. In Jesus' Name.

OTHER AREAS OF SUBMISSION

....

....

....

....

....

....

Submit yourselves, then, to God.
(James 4:7)

FROM THE FATHER'S HEART

I treasure you. You are the apple of My eye! I watch you day and night, always ready to respond to your needs. It gives Me great joy when you come to Me in childlike faith. Do you not know how much it pleases Me to meet your every need? You can call on Me always, in good times and bad. My grace is more than sufficient for you and My power is strongest in your weakness. Lean on Me, My beloved.

PERSONAL WORD FROM MY FATHER

Speak, LORD, for your servant is listening.
(1 Samuel 3:9)

DAY 24

Father, today I'm thankful for:

_____

_____

_____

_____

_____

_____

_____

_____

_____

Meditation

Everyone, without exception, faces opportunities for offense. When I face an opportunity for offense, I can call out to God for help in extending forgiveness just as Jesus extended me forgiveness when He stretched His arms and was nailed to the cross of Calvary. Through God's grace, He forgave me and now, through God's grace, I choose to forgive others. Though I may never receive an apology for the offenses inflicted on my life, I choose to forgive.

May my meditation be pleasing to him, as I rejoice in the LORD.
(Psalm 104:34)

Scripture Focus

Be kind to each other, tenderhearted, forgiving one another,
just as God through Christ has forgiven you.
(Ephesians 4:32, NLT)

FOR REFLECTION

1. What do I believe will result from my unwillingness to forgive others?

2. Reflecting on a past offense, am I harboring any unforgiveness or bitterness in my heart? Explain. List those that come to mind and talk to God about each one.

3. When others have knowingly or unknowingly harmed me, what has been my response? Is there a pattern to my reaction to offense? What adjustments are needed in my attitude when I face opportunities for offense?

4. Matthew 6:14-15 says, "For if you forgive men when they sin against you, your heavenly Father will also forgive you. But if you do not forgive men their sins, your Father will not forgive your sins." What does this mean to me?

_____

_____

_____

_____

_____

_____

Reflect on what I am saying, for the Lord will give you insight into all this.
(2 Timothy 2:7)

REPENTANCE

God of grace, I fall on my knees and ask Your forgiveness. I've sinned against You and sinned against my brothers and sisters by allowing bitterness and resentment to take hold in my heart. I've refused to forgive those who have sinned against me. I've held them captive and as a result, held myself captive. Today, I choose to forgive. Set the captives free, O God. I free my offenders from the penalty due. I ask You not to hold their sin against them. Forgive me, Father. Forgive my offenders. Cleanse me and make me clean again.

OTHER AREAS OF REPENTANCE

_____

_____

_____

_____

Repent, then, and turn to God, so that your sins may be wiped out,
that times of refreshing may come from the Lord.
(Acts 3:19)

SUBMISSION

Lord Jesus, I've been so selfish in the past, demanding to have my way and being overly sensitive to offenses. I've been defensive when accused. I want my attitude to be like Jesus. I want to have an open heart, always ready to forgive. Just as You have forgiven me, I will forgive others. Father, I release every person who has ever brought me harm and free anyone who may harm me in the future. I choose to forgive them now, Lord. Thank You for the price You paid for the forgiveness of my sin, Lord. Praise Your Holy Name. In Jesus' Name.

OTHER AREAS OF SUBMISSION

Submit yourselves, then, to God.
(James 4:7)

FROM THE FATHER'S HEART

I am pleased with you. The grace you offer in granting forgiveness will release grace in your life. When you set others free, you are setting yourself

free. A great price was paid for the forgiveness of your sin and I want you to forgive, always, just as I have forgiven. I offer forgiveness to all and I ask the same of you. Joy will fill you as you walk in the freedom of forgiveness. When you choose forgiveness, you choose life.

PERSONAL WORD FROM MY FATHER

_____

_____

_____

_____

_____

_____

_____

_____

_____

_____

_____

_____

_____

_____

_____

_____

_____

_____

_____

_____

Speak, LORD, for your servant is listening.
(1 Samuel 3:9)

DAY 25

Father, today I'm thankful for:

_____

_____

_____

_____

_____

_____

_____

_____

_____

_____

_____

Meditation

I hear the voice of the Good Shepherd and I know His voice. The devil tempts me to question my ability to hear God's voice and causes me to doubt the ways in which God speaks to my heart. I can trust the voice of the Holy Spirit, who will always lead me into all truth. God's voice and leading will never contradict His Word, but will align with His Word. His Word is truth! I am dependent on God, not on man.

May my meditation be pleasing to him, as I rejoice in the LORD.
(Psalm 104:34)

Scripture Focus

"I am the LORD; that is my name!
I will not give my glory to another or my praise to idols."
(Isaiah 42:8)

FOR REFLECTION

1. How does God speak to me? Do I believe that my Father speaks to me or do I believe He speaks to others only? Explain.

2. To whom do I go when I need answers or counsel? What motivates me to seek them? Have I been required to get my spiritual leader's approval?

3. Does God speak to me through His written Word? Give an example. Does God speak to me through other people? Give an example. Does God speak to me through circumstances? Give an example.

_____

4. Do I rely on my spiritual leaders more or less than I rely on God? Do I need the approval of my spiritual leaders to obey the direction which God is giving me? Why?

_____

Reflect on what I am saying, for the Lord will give you insight into all this.
(2 Timothy 2:7)

REPENTANCE

My God, I have sinned against You! I've erected idols out of man, putting my faith in them instead of You. I've put man on a pedestal, seeking man's direction, though You are the only one with the master plan for my life. Forgive me, Lord, of the sin of idolatry! I'm sorry for following man's voice instead of following Your voice. I demolish my idols today, Lord God, and lift You up. You and You alone, shall I follow.

OTHER AREAS OF REPENTANCE

_____

_____

_____

_____

Repent, then, and turn to God, so that your sins may be wiped out,
that times of refreshing may come from the Lord.
(Acts 3:19)

SUBMISSION

Father God, Jesus is Your beloved Son and My Lord and Savior. I shall listen to Him. I place my life under His authority and ask You to open my ears wide to hear His voice with clarity. I trust that You will lead me and guide me by Your Spirit, keeping me on the path which You have ordained. I love You, Lord, with all of my heart, body, soul and strength. As I walk with You, transform me, mold me and make me into a vessel to bring You glory, honor and praise. In Jesus' Name.

OTHER AREAS OF SUBMISSION

_____

_____

_____

_____

_____

Submit yourselves, then, to God.
(James 4:7)

FROM THE FATHER'S HEART

I am pleased with My Son. Listen to Him. Follow Him. Many voices rally for your attention, trying to speak into your life, but you must silence other voices to hear My Son's voice clearly. As you follow Him and walk in His ways, you will experience the abundant life for which I've made provision. Everything you need is in My Son and everything you need to become is in My Son. Abide in Me and My Son. We shall walk together beside the still waters where you will find peace.

PERSONAL WORD FROM MY FATHER

Speak, LORD, for your servant is listening.
(1 Samuel 3:9)

DAY 26

Father, today I'm thankful for:

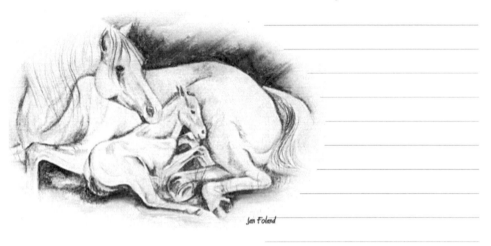

Jan Foland

_____
_____
_____
_____
_____
_____
_____

Meditation

God is at work in my life, even in the midst of my ever-changing circumstances. Regardless of what I face today, God is present in the details, even when I don't realize it. I choose to put on Christ daily, demonstrating a Christ like attitude in the midst of suffering. I can bring hope to others as I radiate the joy of the Lord in spite of my circumstances. As I reach out to bring joy to others, I myself will be blessed.

May my meditation be pleasing to him, as I rejoice in the LORD.
(Psalm 104:34)

Scripture Focus

For I have learned to be content whatever the circumstances. I know what it is to be in need, and I know what it is to have plenty. I have learned the secret of being content in any and every situation, whether well fed or hungry, whether living in plenty or in want. I can do everything through him who gives me strength.
(Philippians 4:11-13)

DAY 26

FOR REFLECTION

1. Have I ever witnessed someone, who daily faces significant challenges, yet maintains a joyful spirit? How would I describe that person?

2. Make contact with the person identified in the previous question. Tell him/her what I've observed and share the impact it's had on my life. Ask him/her to share his/her testimony with me.

3. What physical, spiritual or emotional challenges do I face daily? What has been my attitude about these challenges?

_____

_____

_____

4. In relation to the challenges listed in the previous question, what can I do to help someone else in need? May the Holy Spirit direct me to someone I might bless and reveal how I might bless him/her.

_____

_____

_____

_____

_____

_____

Reflect on what I am saying, for the Lord will give you insight into all this.
(2 Timothy 2:7)

REPENTANCE

Oh God, my God. I put on sackcloth and ashes in repentance. Forgive me for my sin! Though You have blessed me abundantly, I've complained and moaned like a stubborn brat. I've been ungrateful and focused on my suffering instead of being focused on You. I've magnified my problems instead of magnifying You. I need Your mercy once again, Lord. Forgive me!

OTHER AREAS OF REPENTANCE

_____

_____

_____

_____

Repent, then, and turn to God, so that your sins may be wiped out,
that times of refreshing may come from the Lord.
(Acts 3:19)

SUBMISSION

Dear God, although I want what You want, I'm so very weak. Strengthen me for the journey. Strengthen me by Your Spirit in my inner being that I might stand strong in the face of trial. You've blessed me abundantly, O Lord, and I thank You! I surrender to You in the midst of my suffering. Have Your way in me. I trust You to complete the good work You've started in me. My heart belongs to You, my Lord and my God. In Jesus' Name.

OTHER AREAS OF SUBMISSION

_____

_____

_____

_____

_____

_____

Submit yourselves, then, to God.
(James 4:7)

FROM THE FATHER'S HEART

I love you, my little lamb. You are precious in My sight, even when you feel you've failed Me. I love you where you are right now and I will always love you. My love is unconditional and is not dependant on your actions or your faith. My love is unconditional and unchanging. I am your Father. I care for you and love you. Stop striving for My love. My love is yours. Embrace it now.

PERSONAL WORD FROM MY FATHER

_____

_____

_____

_____

_____

_____

_____

_____

_____

_____

_____

_____

_____

_____

_____

_____

_____

_____

_____

_____

_____

_____

_____

_____

_____

Speak, LORD, for your servant is listening.
(I Samuel 3:9)

DAY 27

DATE: _____

Father, today I'm thankful for:

_____
_____
_____
_____
_____
_____
_____
_____
_____
_____
_____
_____

Meditation

My dream was in my Father's heart long before He put it in my heart and only He knows the details of when and how it will be fulfilled. The dream He breathed into my spirit will come to pass, regardless of what others have told me. My Father will prepare me, train me and raise me up to fulfill my dream in His perfect timing. Not before its time, not after its time, but right on time!

May my meditation be pleasing to him, as I rejoice in the LORD.
(Psalm 104:34)

Scripture Focus

You intended to harm me, but God intended it all for good.
He brought me to this position so I could save the lives of many people.
(Genesis 50:20, NLT)

FOR REFLECTION

1. Describe the dream God has given me. When and how did He give me this dream?

    _____

    _____

    _____

    _____

    _____

    _____

2. What has happened since I received this dream? Have I faced anything that challenges my dream or has its fulfillment come to pass without opposition?

    _____

    _____

    _____

    _____

    _____

3. Have I shared my God-given dreams with others? If so, what was their response? Do they support my dream or do they laugh at it? How has another's response affected my feelings about God's dream? Have I allowed others to kill my dream?

    _____

    _____

    _____

_____
_____
_____

4. Have I come into agreement with and submitted myself to God's plan where my dream is concerned? Have I, like the Virgin Mary, said, "Be it unto Me according to what You have said?" Am I willing to allow my Father to bring my dream to pass in spite of the fact that it may seem impossible to me?

_____
_____
_____
_____
_____

Reflect on what I am saying, for the Lord will give you insight into all this.
(2 Timothy 2:7)

REPENTANCE

Mighty God, I've doubted the dream You conceived in my spirit. I've questioned what You've shown me and have wondered how it could possibly come to pass. I feel so unworthy to be used of You, God. Change my heart, Lord God. I'm sorry for questioning that which You've shown me and ask You to forgive me for rejecting what I believe You gave me. Forgive me for my wavering faith, Lord. I'm sorry, Father. I can do nothing without You, but my dream is possible with You.

OTHER AREAS OF REPENTANCE

_____
_____

———————————————————————

———————————————————————

———————————————————————

———————————————————————

Repent, then, and turn to God, so that your sins may be wiped out,
that times of refreshing may come from the Lord.
(Acts 3:19)

SUBMISSION

God, You are the King of kings and Lord of lords! You are the author and the finisher of my faith. I submit myself to Your divinely orchestrated preparation and know that Your plan is for my good and for Your glory. I willingly submit to You, and trust You to make my dream become a reality. Breathe life into that which appears dead. Be it unto me according to what You have said. In Jesus' Name.

OTHER AREAS OF SUBMISSION

———————————————————————

———————————————————————

———————————————————————

———————————————————————

———————————————————————

———————————————————————

Submit yourselves, then, to God.
(James 4:7)

FROM THE FATHER'S HEART

The dream I conceived in your spiritual womb is part of My sovereign plan in the earth. Embrace the dream, as you are My chosen vessel to birth

that which will make My Name great. Without Me, you can do nothing.
Without Me, the dream would surely die. But with Me, it will come to pass
gloriously. I will do it. I, the Giver of Life, will breathe life into others
through the life I've breathed into you.

PERSONAL WORD FROM MY FATHER

_____

_____

_____

_____

_____

_____

_____

_____

_____

_____

_____

_____

_____

_____

_____

_____

_____

_____

_____

_____

_____

_____

Speak, LORD, for your servant is listening.
(1 Samuel 3:9)

DAY 28

DATE: _____

Father, today I'm thankful for:

_____
_____
_____
_____
_____
_____
_____
_____
_____
_____
_____
_____

Meditation

Angels are part of God's wondrous creation, sent to serve and protect God's people. Though I may not see them in the natural realm, they have existed since the beginning and will be present at the end of the age. Although I do not worship angels, I thank God for them and embrace opportunities to see them in action.

May my meditation be pleasing to him, as I rejoice in the LORD.
(Psalm 104:34)

Scripture Focus

Praise the LORD, you his angels, you mighty ones who do his bidding, who obey his word.
Praise the LORD, all his heavenly hosts, you his servants who do his will.
(Psalm 103:20-21)

DAY 28

FOR REFLECTION

1. Do I believe that angels exist? Why or why not? Look up Hebrews 1:14 and memorize it this week. What does this scripture mean to me?

_____

_____

_____

_____

_____

_____

2. Have I experienced an angelic visitation or supernatural protection that cannot be explained in the natural realm? Do I know someone who has witnessed an angelic intervention? Share the experience.

_____

_____

_____

_____

_____

_____

3. Pay close attention to my words today. Am I speaking in line with God's Word, positioning myself for angelic intervention or am I speaking contrary to God's Word, bringing God's angels to a screeching stop?

_____

_____

_____

_____

_____

_____

_____

4. Spend time in praise and thanksgiving for God's protection through angelic beings. Purpose to speak in agreement with God's Word and ask a family member to hold me accountable.

_____

_____

_____

_____

_____

_____

Reflect on what I am saying, for the Lord will give you insight into all this.
(2 Timothy 2:7)

REPENTANCE

God of all creation, instead of being in wonder of Your wondrous mysteries, I've often doubted them. I'm sorry for the ways I've questioned the things I do not understand. At times I seem limited in my humanness, believing only what I can see. Forgive me, Father, for I have sinned. Forgive me, Father, for speaking words contrary to your Word instead of speaking the truth of Your Word to which Your angels hearken.

OTHER AREAS OF REPENTANCE

_____

_____

_____

Repent, then, and turn to God, so that your sins may be wiped out,
that times of refreshing may come from the Lord.
(Acts 3:19)

SUBMISSION

Father God, You are so good to me. Thank You for releasing guardian angels who hearken to Your voice to protect and serve me, even when I'm not aware of their presence. I surrender my tongue to You, Father; take control of my mouth. Enable me, Lord, to speak only words that are in agreement with Your Holy Word. May I hearken to Your voice and speak Your Word so Your angels can hearken to Your voice and act upon Your Word to bring Your divine plan to pass. In Jesus' Name.

OTHER AREAS OF SUBMISSION

Submit yourselves, then, to God.
(James 4:7)

FROM THE FATHER'S HEART

I AM watching over you always, My faithful servant. I guard your ways and protect your path, even when you are unaware. My angels are round

about you always, listening to My commands and responding to My voice. I want you, My child, to listen to My commands and respond to My voice too. As you listen to Me and walk in My ways, I will open your spiritual eyes even wider to witness and proclaim the wondrous work of My hand.

PERSONAL WORD FROM MY FATHER

_____

_____

_____

_____

_____

_____

_____

_____

_____

_____

_____

_____

_____

_____

_____

_____

_____

_____

_____

_____

Speak, LORD, for your servant is listening.
(1 Samuel 3:9)

DAY 29

DATE: _____

Father, today I'm thankful for:

_____
_____
_____
_____
_____
_____
_____
_____
_____
_____

Meditation

My wise Father blessed me with the privilege of choosing the people with whom I develop a relationship. I am influenced by my relationships and my relationship with others influences them. God does not require me to engage in a relationship with everyone who crosses my path. As I seek wisdom from my Father, He will help me establish the relationships He desires, to fulfill His purpose.

May my meditation be pleasing to him, as I rejoice in the LORD.
(Psalm 104:34)

Scripture Focus

Make allowance for each other's faults, and forgive anyone who offends you.
Remember, the Lord forgave you, so you must forgive others.
(Colossians 3:13, NLT)

FOR REFLECTION

I.   From my perspective, what is the difference between "love" and "like"?

_____

_____

_____

_____

_____

_____

2.   As I think of someone I like, why do I like him/her? As I think of someone I don't like, why don't I like him/her?

_____

_____

_____

_____

_____

_____

3.   Are there any people in my circle of relationships with whom I've felt obligated to maintain a relationship, yet it seems to be a constant struggle to maintain that relationship?

_____

_____

_____

_____

_____

_____

4. As I examine my circle of friends, how much time am I investing in these relationships? Is the effort I'm putting into these relationships producing fruitful results? If not, what is being produced in these relationships?

_____

_____

_____

_____

_____

Reflect on what I am saying, for the Lord will give you insight into all this.
(2 Timothy 2:7)

REPENTANCE

O God, You have opened my eyes today. I've made poor choices in relationships and misinterpreted Your desire for me to forgive. I see now that although You require me to forgive those who have sinned against me, You don't require me to continue a relationship with those who bring me harm. I'm sorry for my failings. Forgive me for my sin, Lord God. Forgive me for my ignorance and poor judgment. Thank You, Father, for the blood of Your Son, shed for the forgiveness of sin. Cleanse me now, loving Father, from my sin.

OTHER AREAS OF REPENTANCE

_____

_____

_____

_____

_____

*Repent, then, and turn to God, so that your sins may be wiped out,
that times of refreshing may come from the Lord.*
(Acts 3:19)

SUBMISSION

Here I am, Holy Lord. I want You to have Your way in every area of my life. I bring to You all of my relationships. I lay them before You now and ask that You would establish those relationships that are built on Your purpose, those that will draw me closer to You. I give You permission to remove relationships that might take me away from You or hinder Your purpose in my life. Thank You God, for the privilege of choosing relationships. Please choose my relationships for me, dear Lord. In Jesus' Name.

OTHER AREAS OF SUBMISSION

_____

_____

_____

_____

_____

Submit yourselves, then, to God.
(James 4:7)

FROM THE FATHER'S HEART

I love you with My unfailing love and want you to love others. I have poured My love into your heart by My Holy Spirit and you shall pour out that love to others. I forgave you through the shed blood of My Beloved Son, and I want you to pour out My forgiveness to others, even those you do not like. I shall establish the relationships ordained of Me and will send the roots down deep so you can grow and flourish in Me. Make Me the center of your relationships and I shall lead and guide you to great abundance.

PERSONAL WORD FROM MY FATHER

Speak, LORD, for your servant is listening.
(1 Samuel 3:9)

DAY 30

Father, today I'm thankful for:

_____

_____

_____

_____

_____

_____

_____

_____

_____

Meditation

Although I will face many opportunities for suffering, I can choose to trust God in the midst of suffering, knowing that He has a perfectly orchestrated plan. For the joy set before Him, He endured the cross for me. For the joy set before me, I will endure my seasons of suffering for the good of others and for God's glory, even when I don't understand.

May my meditation be pleasing to him, as I rejoice in the LORD.
(Psalm 104:34)

Scripture Focus

"Now my heart is troubled, and what shall I say? 'Father, save me from this hour'?
No, it was for this very reason I came to this hour.
(John 12:27)

FOR REFLECTION

1. As I picture the suffering Jesus endured on the cross of Calvary, what does His crucifixion, death and resurrection mean to me? What does the statement, "For the joy set before Him, He endured the cross" mean to me?

_____

_____

_____

_____

_____

2. Have I ever been desperate for deliverance from my physical, emotional or spiritual suffering? What resulted from my suffering? Have I wondered why I had to endure this season of pain? Talk to My Father about this experience. What did He reveal to me?

_____

_____

_____

_____

_____

3. Thinking especially of loved ones, have I ever stepped in to deliver anyone from his or her suffering? Explain. Was my intervention motivated by God? What resulted from my intervention?

_____

_____

_____

_____

_____

_____

_____

4. Thinking of an experience I witnessed when someone endured intense
    suffering that resulted in good for them and for others, in the end, how
    did it bring glory to God?

_____

_____

_____

_____

_____

_____

Reflect on what I am saying, for the Lord will give you insight into all this.
(2 Timothy 2:7)

REPENTANCE

Lord God, my suffering seems unbearable at times and I've become
bitter when I cry out to You for deliverance and You don't seem to respond.
I've demonstrated a rebellious attitude when I've watched my loved ones
suffer too, and felt as if You didn't care. I'm so sorry, righteous Father, for
the attitude of my heart. Take out this heart of stone and give me a heart of
flesh. Renew a right spirit within me, God.

OTHER AREAS OF REPENTANCE

_____

_____

_____

Repent, then, and turn to God, so that your sins may be wiped out,
that times of refreshing may come from the Lord.
(Acts 3:19)

SUBMISSION

Lord Jesus, Lamb of God, You endured unimaginable suffering for the forgiveness of my sin so that I could be whole. Thank You, God, for Your great demonstration of love. Now Lord, I submit my life fully to You. Have Your way in me. Accomplish what You need to accomplish in me. Strengthen me by Your Spirit in my inner being to endure this season and use my life and my suffering to minister hope and healing to others. In Jesus' Name.

OTHER AREAS OF SUBMISSION

Submit yourselves, then, to God.
(James 4:7)

FROM THE FATHER'S HEART

You are precious to Me, and My love for you will never change. Your willingness to lay down your life according to My perfect will delights Me. Your suffering will not be in vain, My beloved. Your pain will not endure forever, but My love for you surely will endure forever. Trust Me to take you through this season and receive My peace as we continue the journey. In the midst of your suffering, offer Me the sacrifice of praise, for the victory belongs to you!

PERSONAL WORD FROM MY FATHER

_____

_____

_____

_____

_____

_____

_____

_____

_____

_____

_____

_____

_____

_____

_____

_____

_____

_____

_____

_____

_____

_____

Speak, LORD, for your servant is listening.
(1 Samuel 3:9)

DAY 31

Father, today I'm thankful for:

_____

_____

_____

_____

_____

_____

_____

_____

_____

Meditation

Although the enemy has brought much destruction, tearing down that which is sacred in my life, God will restore what the enemy has destroyed. With God, all things are possible! When the manifestation of His restoration comes to pass, all will know that no man could have brought it to pass. Even those who have mocked and ridiculed the work of Your hand, will stand in awe of what You have done. The one and only true God will receive all glory, all honor and all praise.

May my meditation be pleasing to him, as I rejoice in the LORD.
(Psalm 104:34)

Scripture Focus

They realized this work had been done with the help of our God.
(Nehemiah 6:16, NLT)

FOR REFLECTION

1. What area of my life has been torn down and is in need of rebuilding? Consider family, friends, relationships, career, and emotional, physical and spiritual issues. Identify and document what has taken place and what is needed for rebuilding.

    _____

    _____

    _____

    _____

    _____

2. Regardless of the cause for the past destruction, have I shared my heart with my Father about what has been destroyed and have I forgiven those involved? Am I willing to be used by God for restoration?

    _____

    _____

    _____

    _____

    _____

3. As I set some time aside to process the emotions related to the above area, can I repent for the part I played in the destruction? Can I stand in the gap and ask God's forgiveness for others involved, including past generations? Repent before the Lord, ask Him to restore that which has been broken, and make myself available for the heavenly rebuilding project.

    _____

    _____

_____

_____

_____

_____

4. Do I believe God can restore what has been destroyed in the past? Am I willing to move forward in spite of mockers and those who doubt and ridicule me? Make God's restoration a matter of daily prayer, and ask God for wisdom regularly. He hears my prayer and is already at work on my behalf. Expect to see Him at work!

_____

_____

_____

_____

_____

Reflect on what I am saying, for the Lord will give you insight into all this.
(2 Timothy 2:7)

REPENTANCE

God of all power and might, though I've been surrounded by destruction, I've failed to bring my concerns to You. Instead of asking You to bring restoration to that which has been left in ruins, I've complained. Instead of making myself available to You as a vessel to bring restoration, I've stood far off, assuming all had been lost. Dear God, forgive my sin! Forgive the error of my ways! I lay prostrate before You in Repentance. I'm sorry, Father.

OTHER AREAS OF REPENTANCE

_____

_____

_____

_____

_____

_____

Repent, then, and turn to God, so that your sins may be wiped out,
that times of refreshing may come from the Lord.
(Acts 3:19)

SUBMISSION

O Lord, Most High God, I grieve at what the enemy has torn down in my life. Yet in spite of the loss, I believe that all things are possible with You. Lord, I kneel at Your throne, and ask You to rebuild and restore that which has been stolen. I make myself available to be used of You during the process of rebuilding. Send me as part of Your answer. Use me, Father, my life belongs to You. In Jesus' Name.

OTHER AREAS OF SUBMISSION

_____

_____

_____

_____

_____

_____

Submit yourselves, then, to God.
(James 4:7)

FROM THE FATHER'S HEART

I am the God of restoration and nothing is impossible for Me. I have waited for you to release that which appears to lie in ruins. Bring everything to Me, my trusted servant, even the broken pieces and the ashes. I will restore all things, turning your brokenness and ashes into a beautiful master-piece that radiates My glory. As you build the foundation of your life on Me, nothing can shake you as you will be standing firm on the Solid Rock.

PERSONAL WORD FROM MY FATHER

Speak, LORD, for your servant is listening.
(1 Samuel 3:9)

DATE: _____

DAY 32

Father, today I'm thankful for:

_____

_____

_____

_____

_____

_____

_____

_____

_____

Meditation

When I submit to and commit to God's plan, I will face opportunities to become distracted. As I move forward in my Father's work, some may mock me, lie to me, lie about me, deceive me or manipulate me. I refuse to engage in skirmishes with the enemy. With my Father's help, I remain focused on His purpose, and with great joy I will complete the tasks He has given me. All will see that He is the God who makes the impossible possible.

May my meditation be pleasing to him, as I rejoice in the LORD.
(Psalm 104:34)

Scripture Focus

So I replied by sending this message to them: "I am engaged in a great work, so I can't come. Why should I stop working to come and meet with you?"
Four times they sent the same message and each time I gave the same reply.
(Nehemiah 6:3-4, NLT)

DAY 32

FOR REFLECTION

1. Reflecting on the building project identified in the Day 31 devotion, as I engage in God's rebuilding project, the enemy may attempt to distract me by luring me into senseless skirmishes. What possible distractions are ahead that could become stumbling blocks? Identify them.

2. In relation to the issues addressed in question #1, how can I prepare myself ahead of time to defuse these distractions if and when they present themselves?

3. Looking back, think of a time I became distracted while in the midst of fulfilling an assignment God had given me. Explain.

---

4. What was the outcome of my distraction? How much time, if any, was wasted? How can I avoid taking the devil's bait when he sets his schemes in motion to take my focus off of God and the project with which He has entrusted me?

Reflect on what I am saying, for the Lord will give you insight into all this.
(2 Timothy 2:7)

REPENTANCE

My Lord and my God, I fall on my knees with a heavy heart. At times I have willingly accepted the tasks You have given me, started strong, then finished weak, if at all. Forgive me for my unfaithfulness. Forgive me for taking Satan's bait, becoming snared in his schemes to distract me from Your purpose. I'm sorry for sinning against You, dear Lord. Cleanse me and wash away my sin so I might start anew.

OTHER AREAS OF REPENTANCE

_Repent, then, and turn to God, so that your sins may be wiped out,
that times of refreshing may come from the Lord._
(Acts 3:19)

SUBMISSION

O, Father, I'm grateful that You are the God of second chances. Thank You for not giving up on me in spite of my past failures. As You continue reconstruction work in my life, I ask that You would align my heart with Your heart. Grant me wisdom, Lord of Hosts, and discernment to recognize distractions that strive to woo me away from Your plans and purposes. Enable me by Your Spirit to remain steadfast, focused on what You've asked of me, and unmoved by man's misguided words or actions. In Jesus' Name.

OTHER AREAS OF SUBMISSION

Submit yourselves, then, to God.
(James 4:7)

FROM THE FATHER'S HEART

I grant abundant wisdom and discernment to you, Child, so walk therefore in it. Though opposition will come to drive you away from My work, I will keep your spiritual eyes open wide to recognize it. I will show you wolves clothed as sheep and will reveal schemes of the enemy, which come in many forms. Your eyes will be kept wide open as you keep your heart open wide to Me. As you walk with Me, nothing can delay or destroy what I am building.

PERSONAL WORD FROM MY FATHER

_____

_____

_____

_____

_____

_____

_____

_____

_____

_____

_____

_____

_____

_____

_____

_____

_____

_____

_____

_____

Speak, LORD, for your servant is listening.
(1 Samuel 3:9)

DAY 33

Father, today I'm thankful for:

_____

_____

_____

_____

_____

_____

_____

_____

_____

_____

Meditation

Regardless of where I am today, the great I AM, the God and Father of the Lord Jesus, desires fellowship with me. Whether I have sinned or have been deceived by the devil, my heavenly Father is waiting for my return. If I have drifted away, I can drift back into His arms today. Jesus, the spotless Lamb of God, made the way for my relationship to be restored with my loving Father.

May my meditation be pleasing to him, as I rejoice in the LORD.
(Psalm 104:34)

Scripture Focus

We must pay more careful attention, therefore,
to what we have heard, so that we do not drift away.
(Hebrews 2:1)

FOR REFLECTION

1. Have I ever been duped by the devil? Explain the circumstances that led to this experience. Pay particular attention to the presence or lack of presence of peace during that time.

2. Have I ever experienced a season where I drifted away from God? Did it happen suddenly or was it so gradual that I wasn't consciously aware of it? Explain.

3. How did I eventually recognize and acknowledge that I had drifted from God? Am I drifting now? Is shame from unconfessed sin keeping me from approaching God?

_____

_____

_____

_____

4. Am I anchored in Jesus? Am I planted in Christian fellowship where I can grow and find accountability? If not, ask God to lead me by His Spirit where I belong. If I'm not certain, visit various functions and churches. God will make His plan clear as I move forward.

_____

_____

_____

_____

_____

Reflect on what I am saying, for the Lord will give you insight into all this.
(2 Timothy 2:7)

REPENTANCE

I confess my sin to You, Lord God. I have no excuses. I cannot justify my errors. I have drifted away from You, Father. I admit it. I've been duped by the devil and have fallen away from You. I'm sorry, my Lord and Savior. I want to return to You now. I've backslidden, but now I want to slide back into Your arms. Rescue me again, Father, for my sin has been great. I draw near to You now, Father. Draw near to me. I need You more than ever.

OTHER AREAS OF REPENTANCE

_____

_____

_____

....

....

....

....

Repent, then, and turn to God, so that your sins may be wiped out,
that times of refreshing may come from the Lord.
(Acts 3:19)

SUBMISSION

Lord Jesus, though I have been ashamed of my poor behavior, You love me in spite of my behavior. I'm amazed that You love me 100%, even when I have failed. Your love is unchanging and I'm so grateful that You receive me when I don't deserve it. Though I've failed in so many ways, I ask that You would use my life to bring You glory. Though I've fallen into the enemy's traps, please use me to help others avoid the snares I've encountered. In Jesus' Name.

OTHER AREAS OF SUBMISSION

....

....

....

....

....

....

Submit yourselves, then, to God.
(James 4:7)

FROM THE FATHER'S HEART

I shall use you, My Beloved. What you consider failings are no surprise to Me. I saw your entire life before it began. I know You better than you know yourself. What you may consider failures are opportunities for My glory to shine before man. What you may consider mistakes are opportunities for My grace and mercy to be displayed. Let me lift your shame, for the price has been paid. I love you, 100%. I always have and always will. That is who I AM.

PERSONAL WORD FROM MY FATHER

Speak, LORD, for your servant is listening.
(1 Samuel 3:9)

DAY 34

Father, today I'm thankful for:

_____
_____
_____
_____
_____
_____
_____
_____
_____

Meditation

The greatest treasures I will ever discover on the earth are the treasures discovered in the darkness. Though I cannot explain it, I know in my heart that the most precious jewels emerge from the most difficult seasons of my life, if my heart is turned toward my Father. I can embrace Jesus in the darkness, knowing that He will give me treasures to bring new life to others.

May my meditation be pleasing to him, as I rejoice in the LORD.
(Psalm 104:34)

Scripture Focus

I will give you the treasures of darkness, riches stored in secret places, that you may know that I am the LORD, the God of Israel, who summons you by name.
(Isaiah 45:3)

FOR REFLECTION

1. As I review my wilderness season, what treasures have I discovered this far into the journey?

2. Have I ever lost something that was precious to me? Explain. Did I find it or did I have to confront feelings of loss? How do I view this loss now?

3. What do I consider my treasures on this earth? With an open heart, what is most important to me?

_____

_____

4. What am I searching for? As I identify the desires of my heart, share them with my Father and ask Him to give me the desires of my heart.

_____

_____

_____

_____

_____

_____

_____

Reflect on what I am saying, for the Lord will give you insight into all this.
(2 Timothy 2:7)

REPENTANCE

Father, I bow before You, acknowledging that I know so little about Your ways. I've begged to be delivered from this season of wilderness, yet I realize that You are doing much more than I realize, bringing change in me that is necessary to fulfill Your plan. Change me, Father. I'm no longer desperate to be delivered from my suffering, I'm desperate to become what You want me to become. Mold me. Make me into that which will bring glory to You.

OTHER AREAS OF REPENTANCE

_____

_____

_____

_____

_____

Repent, then, and turn to God, so that your sins may be wiped out,
that times of refreshing may come from the Lord.
(Acts 3:19)

SUBMISSION

Here I am, Father. I am here for You. I turn away from my ways, knowing my ways are not the path that leads to Your abundant life. I turn to You. I give myself to You for Your use. I am here, offering myself as a living sacrifice. Make me holy and acceptable to You. In Jesus' Name.

OTHER AREAS OF SUBMISSION

Submit yourselves, then, to God.
(James 4:7)

FROM THE FATHER'S HEART

You are My greatest treasure. You are the apple of My eye. Do you know how much I love you? Do you know how much I search for you every moment of every day? I long for you. I love you! I have hidden treasures for you. Seek Me with all of your heart and you will discover the jewels of My righteousness and the glory of My presence. Receive My love!

PERSONAL WORD FROM MY FATHER

Speak, LORD, for your servant is listening.
(1 Samuel 3:9)

DAY 35

Father, today I'm thankful for:

_____

_____

_____

_____

_____

_____

_____

_____

_____

_____

_____

Jan Friend

Meditation

If I am willing, I AM will accomplish wondrous works during my sojourn on earth. If I make myself available for whatever He desires, I make myself a tool in the Master's hand, something through which He can accomplish great and mighty works. Without Him, I can do nothing, but with Him nothing is impossible!

May my meditation be pleasing to him, as I rejoice in the LORD.
(Psalm 104:34)

Scripture Focus

"I am the Lord's servant," Mary answered. "May it be to me as you have said."
(Luke 1:38)

FOR REFLECTION

1. What has God asked of me? What has He put on my heart to do? Paying particular attention to the things I may consider trivial or of little value, document what I believe God wants me to do.

_____

_____

_____

_____

_____

_____

2. Have I submitted to that which I believe God desires from me? What, if anything, stands in the way of my submission?

_____

_____

_____

_____

_____

_____

3. Do I understand why God is asking me to do this? If not, do I need to understand the details before I can say, "May it be to me as You have said"?

_____

_____

_____

_____

_____

_____

_____

4. God is sovereign and chooses the vessels through which He will fulfill His plan. Am I prepared to be a willing vessel? Am I afraid to surrender all so He can do what He desires to do through me? I can share my fears with my Father. What did He speak to my heart?

_____

_____

_____

_____

_____

_____

Reflect on what I am saying, for the Lord will give you insight into all this.
(2 Timothy 2:7)

REPENTANCE

My Creator, how I've limited You through my stubborn refusal to believe that You could do something with my life. I'm sorry, Father, for trying to put You in a box and trying to limit what You could or could not do with me. You are the Potter, I am the clay. I've failed! Help me, dear God, to remember who You are and that I am Yours to form into that which will bring You honor.

OTHER AREAS OF REPENTANCE

_____

_____

_____

_____

_____

_____

Repent, then, and turn to God, so that your sins may be wiped out,
that times of refreshing may come from the Lord.
(Acts 3:19)

SUBMISSION

Oh Lord, nothing is impossible with You! I am so limited in every way. But when I am weak, You are strong. When I am a failure, You make me a victor! When I am weary, You bring me strength. Fill me to overflowing, Father God, with everything I need for life and godliness. I can live life to the fullest only through You! In Jesus' Name.

OTHER AREAS OF SUBMISSION

_____

_____

_____

_____

_____

_____

Submit yourselves, then, to God.
(James 4:7)

FROM THE FATHER'S HEART

You are My chosen one. I have raised you up for such a time as this. I have equipped you with everything you need to fulfill My divine plan. As you submit yourself to Me, I do the work. I will fill you, do you not know by now? You can do all things through Me! Nobody on the earth, not one, can fulfill that which I have called you to fulfill. Go for it, My child. For I am with you!

PERSONAL WORD FROM MY FATHER

Speak, LORD, for your servant is listening.
(1 Samuel 3:9)

DAY 36

Father, today I'm thankful for:

_____

_____

_____

_____

_____

_____

_____

_____

_____

_____

Meditation

My Father is trustworthy. He is the author and finisher of my faith. He is the Alpha and the Omega. He is awesome in every way! I can put my trust in Him regardless of what trials visit my life. He is faithful. Always. He loves me. Always. If I know His love, I can trust Him and if I trust Him, I can rest in Him.

May my meditation be pleasing to him, as I rejoice in the LORD.
(Psalm 104:34)

Scripture Focus

You watched me as I was being formed in utter seclusion, as I was woven together in the dark of the womb. You saw me before I was born. Every day of my life was recorded in your book. Every moment was laid out before a single day had passed.
(Psalm 139:15-16, NLT)

FOR REFLECTION

1. As I reflect on the more difficult challenges of my life, were any of these trials a blessing in disguise? Explain.

_____

_____

_____

_____

_____

_____

2. What was my attitude when faced with the challenges I mentioned?

_____

_____

_____

_____

_____

_____

3. What did I learn, if anything, from walking through the most difficult seasons of my life? Did I draw closer to God or did I drift further from Him? Why?

_____

_____

_____

_____

4. When I face trial, am I willing to trust God in spite of my circumstances? Why or why not?

Reflect on what I am saying, for the Lord will give you insight into all this.
(2 Timothy 2:7)

REPENTANCE

God, my God, how often I have thought that You had forsaken me! Yet in my darkest moments, You were there and You had a plan. Forgive me for stressing and wavering in my faith when trials confronted me. When all is well, it is so easy to trust You, but when trial comes, it hasn't been so easy for me. Help me develop my faith, Lord. I need You.

OTHER AREAS OF REPENTANCE

Repent, then, and turn to God, so that your sins may be wiped out,
that times of refreshing may come from the Lord.
(Acts 3:19)

SUBMISSION

Lord Jesus, Giver of Life, I put my trust in You today. Regardless of what circumstances I will face today, I choose to give them to You, to trust You and to rest in You. Your love enables me to trust You. Thank You for loving me. Thank You for walking with me through the valley of the shadow of death. I can rest knowing You are with me, and will never leave me or forsake me. In Jesus' Name.

OTHER AREAS OF SUBMISSION

Submit yourselves, then, to God.
(James 4:7)

FROM THE FATHER'S HEART

You are safe under the shadow of My wing. Nothing can take place in your life without it being filtered through Me. I am well aware of every detail. I have a plan for what you face today and I have a plan for what you will face tomorrow. My plan is a good plan. You can rest in Me because I love you! Everything is going be ok!

PERSONAL WORD FROM MY FATHER

Speak, LORD, for your servant is listening.
(1 Samuel 3:9)

DAY 37

DATE: _____

Father, today I'm thankful for:

_____

_____

_____

_____

_____

_____

_____

_____

_____

_____

Meditation

My God, my God, You have not forsaken me! I rejoice today that my Lord and Savior paved the way for my emotional, physical and spiritual healing. I receive it by faith now. Today I am set free! Today I am healed. Today, my wounds are healed by the wounds Jesus endured for my sake. I receive it today!

May my meditation be pleasing to him, as I rejoice in the LORD.
(Psalm 104:34)

Scripture Focus

He heals the brokenhearted and binds up their wounds.
(Psalm 147:3)

FOR REFLECTION

1. What price did Jesus pay for my freedom from sin, sickness, disease, shame, and sorrow? What penalty was paid for my peace?

_____

_____

_____

_____

_____

_____

2. Have I received God's gift in Jesus? When did I receive His gift? Explain the details. If I have not received Jesus and the gift of eternal life through the forgiveness of my sin, do I want to receive it now? I can repent of my sin right now and invite Him into my heart to dwell forever.

_____

_____

_____

_____

_____

3. Do I have unhealed wounds from the past? Am I willing to allow Jesus to touch those wounds now? I can invite Him to heal my wounds and accept the path to healing that He has planned for me. I am free! I am healed!

_____

_____

_____

_____

_____

_____

4. Thank God for the gift of His Son! Thank You, Father, for the healing
    You have brought to my life through the blood of Your only begotten
    Son. Thank You for past healing, the healing You are doing today and
    the healing that will come in the future.

_____

_____

_____

_____

_____

Reflect on what I am saying, for the Lord will give you insight into all this.
(2 Timothy 2:7)

REPENTANCE

Will You forgive me, Father, once again? How many times I have come
to You for forgiveness, yet here I am again. I am in awe that Your mercy is
new every morning. I have taken You for granted. I have taken the sacrifice
Jesus made for me for granted. Oh God, what a price He paid for my
freedom from the penalty of sin! I'm sorry God, I'm so sorry for grieving
Your heart as I have. Cleanse me, Father. Wash my sin away so I might
stand in the righteousness You provided at Calvary.

OTHER AREAS OF REPENTANCE

_____

_____

_____

_____

_____

_____

Repent, then, and turn to God, so that your sins may be wiped out,
that times of refreshing may come from the Lord.
(Acts 3:19)

SUBMISSION

Fill my heart with understanding of the price Your Son paid for my freedom. Enable me to live a life demonstrating that understanding and drawing others to the cross. You have saved me from the penalty of my sinfulness. You have given me freedom and liberty. You have set me free and I am free indeed. Use me now, Lord God, to lead the lost to You, the only source of hope. In Jesus' Name.

OTHER AREAS OF SUBMISSION

_____

_____

_____

_____

_____

Submit yourselves, then, to God.
(James 4:7)

FROM THE FATHER'S HEART

I so loved you that I sent My Son to save you. How I long for you to know the fullness of My love. As you walk with Me, and write My Word on the tablet of your heart to lead and guide you, the understanding you desire will increase. The price My Son paid on your behalf was a great price indeed, but it was paid willingly with My love for I AM love.

PERSONAL WORD FROM MY FATHER

Speak, LORD, for your servant is listening.
(1 Samuel 3:9)

DAY 38

DATE: _____

Father, today I'm thankful for:

_____
_____
_____
_____
_____
_____
_____
_____
_____
_____

Meditation

It is as important for me to obey God when He directs me to stand still as it is to obey when He directs me to take action. I hear the voice of my Good Shepherd. I know His voice and I will follow Him. I can and will be still and know He is God.

May my meditation be pleasing to him, as I rejoice in the LORD.
(Psalm 104:34)

Scripture Focus

Enter his gates with thanksgiving; go into his courts with praise.
Give thanks to him and praise his name.
(Psalm 100:4, NLT)

186

DAY 38

FOR REFLECTION

1. Am I in a jam? Explain.

2. Have I asked God for direction? Have I asked Him for wisdom? If so, what has He directed me to do? I can talk to my Father about my situation and ask Him for His plan and strategy. What has the Lord revealed to me?

3. Has God asked me now, or has He ever directed me to stand still when all walls seem to be closing in on me? Did I obey? What happened as a result of my obedience or disobedience?

_____

_____

_____

4. What does, "This battle belongs to the Lord" mean to me? If my battle belongs to the Lord, am I willing to stand still?

_____

_____

_____

_____

_____

Reflect on what I am saying, for the Lord will give you insight into all this.
(2 Timothy 2:7)

REPENTANCE

Father God, my wondrous God! You have opened my eyes to see where I've gone wrong. How often I have launched into action when Your desire was for me to stand still and how often I've stood still when I should have responded to Your call to action. I'm sorry, Lord, for taking matters into my own hands when You wanted to take matters into Your able hands. Only You know what is best, Lord. I want to go when You want me to go and stand still when You want me to be still. God Almighty, I have failed without You and cannot do this without Your help. Help me, O God!

OTHER AREAS OF REPENTANCE

_____

_____

_____

_____

_____

_____

_____

Repent, then, and turn to God, so that your sins may be wiped out,
that times of refreshing may come from the Lord.
(Acts 3:19)

SUBMISSION

Holy Lord, You know the best way. You know the only way to life abundant. I want Your plan. I want Your strategy. I surrender my strategies and plans to You, acknowledging that I do not know the best way in which to act. When You tell me to "Go" I will go and when You tell me to "stand still" I will stand still. My battles belong to You, Most High God. Give me Your battle plans, Lord, and I will follow. In Jesus' Name.

OTHER AREAS OF SUBMISSION

_____

_____

_____

_____

_____

_____

Submit yourselves, then, to God.
(James 4:7)

FROM THE FATHER'S HEART

I protect you because I love you. My love for you is outrageous. My love is radical! I always have your best interest in mind. At times I will ask you to move and I delight when you move. But at times I will ask you to step aside and do nothing but trust Me. When I ask you to stand still, obey My voice. As you obey Me, you will see the wondrous works of My hand. Do not fear the enemies before you. When your enemies arise, I will act on your behalf, and your enemies will be scattered.

PERSONAL WORD FROM MY FATHER

Speak, LORD, for your servant is listening.
(1 Samuel 3:9)

DAY 39

Father, today I'm thankful for:

_____

_____

_____

_____

_____

_____

_____

_____

_____

_____

Meditation

God will take everything the enemy meant for evil and use it for my good, the good of others, and for His glory. I need not be ashamed of my seasons of suffering but can rejoice in God's faithfulness throughout my trials. As I share my testimony of the comfort God gave me, it brings comfort to others. The God of all comfort will use me to bring comfort to others, if I am willing.

May my meditation be pleasing to him, as I rejoice in the LORD.
(Psalm 104:34)

Scripture Focus

Praise be to the God and Father of our Lord Jesus Christ, the Father of compassion and the God of all comfort, who comforts us in all our troubles, so that we can comfort those in any trouble with the comfort we ourselves have received from God. For just as the sufferings of Christ flow over into our lives, so also through Christ our comfort overflows.
(2 Corinthians 1:3-5)

FOR REFLECTION

1. What area of major suffering have I endured and found victory through Christ? Explain.

_____

_____

_____

_____

_____

_____

_____

2. Am I willing to openly share my journey through suffering addressed in question #1? If I have encountered others facing similar circumstances, have I taken the opportunity to share my testimony?

_____

_____

_____

_____

_____

_____

_____

3. If I have hesitated to share my testimony, am I ashamed to reveal my experience or do I fear others will view me as weak? What needs to happen in order for me to be free to share my story?

_____

_____

_____

_____

_____

_____

_____

4. What is the primary message written on the chalkboard of my heart? Does the message reveal the heart of God or does it reveal lies of the enemy? If issues of shame or rejection are written on my chalkboard, ask God to erase them by His Spirit and to replace them with His message of love.

_____

_____

_____

_____

_____

_____

Reflect on what I am saying, for the Lord will give you insight into all this.
(2 Timothy 2:7)

REPENTANCE

God, I have been selfish in keeping my testimony hidden. You delivered me, yet I've kept silent about You, my Deliverer! I've feared that revealing the areas with which I've struggled might make me appear weak or unstable to others. Pride has gripped me, Father, and though I didn't see it before, I see it clearly now. As I humble myself before You, please wipe away my sin. Forgive me of my sin, O Lord.

OTHER AREAS OF REPENTANCE

_____

_____

_____

_____

_____

_____

Repent, then, and turn to God, so that your sins may be wiped out,
that times of refreshing may come from the Lord.
(Acts 3:19)

SUBMISSION

Holy Father, thank You for walking with me through the wilderness seasons. As I ponder Your greatness, I stand in awe of You, wondrous God. You've had compassion on me and have comforted me, even when I didn't know You were there and didn't deserve Your attention. I am willing, Lord, to share the testimony of Your goodness to anyone You bring across my path. As You open the door for me to share, I am ready in season and out. Use me to comfort others with the comfort You have given me. In Jesus' Name.

OTHER AREAS OF SUBMISSION

_____

_____

_____

_____

_____

_____

Submit yourselves, then, to God.
(James 4:7)

FROM THE FATHER'S HEART

I am always here to comfort you. My love for you and for others motivates compassion and comfort. All of heaven stands at attention when My

Name is being honored. You bring honor to My Name as You tell others what I have done for you. Let Me fill you with My love. Let Me fill you with My compassion. Let Me fill you with My comfort. Now go, pour out what I have poured into you, into others. Then come, My child, and let Me fill you more.

PERSONAL WORD FROM MY FATHER

Speak, LORD, for your servant is listening.
(1 Samuel 3:9)

DATE: _____

DAY 40

Father, today I'm thankful for:

_____

_____

_____

_____

_____

_____

_____

_____

_____

Meditation

I do not know the day or the hour of Jesus' return, nor do I know the day or the hour my life on earth will come to a close. I will live every day as if it is my last and will make every moment matter.

May my meditation be pleasing to him, as I rejoice in the LORD.
(Psalm 104:34)

Scripture Focus

"Yes, I am coming soon." Amen. Come, Lord Jesus.
(Revelation 22:20)

DAY 40

FOR REFLECTION

1. If I died today, am I confident that I would spend eternity with my Father in heaven? Why or why not? Explain.

_____

_____

_____

_____

_____

_____

_____

2. Do I fear the return of Jesus or do I anticipate it with joy and peace? Why or why not? Explain.

_____

_____

_____

_____

_____

_____

_____

3. If Jesus returned today, am I ready for His return? Why or why not? What do I need to do to prepare myself for His return?

_____

_____

_____

_____

_____

_____

4. If I had only one week left on earth, would I live differently than I do now? Do I need to ask someone's forgiveness or forgive others? Have I done what I believe God has asked of me? If not, what has been left undone? List what comes to the surface as I ponder these issues and act on what God has revealed to me.

_____

_____

_____

_____

_____

_____

Reflect on what I am saying, for the Lord will give you insight into all this.
(2 Timothy 2:7)

REPENTANCE

Master, I often forget that life on earth is but a tiny slice of time and that eternity is forever. I'm sorry, Lord Jesus, for living my life so recklessly, making issues of things that don't matter and not making issues of things that do matter. I need to change, Lord. Help me to change and renew my mind so that I can make a difference in Your Kingdom. Help me prepare my heart and life for Jesus' return.

OTHER AREAS OF REPENTANCE

_____

_____

_____

Repent, then, and turn to God, so that your sins may be wiped out,
that times of refreshing may come from the Lord.
(Acts 3:19)

SUBMISSION

Father God, only You know the hour of Your Son's return. I receive Jesus today, and will receive Him every day anew, knowing that because of Him, I will spend eternity with You. I submit myself to You, Lord, and ask You to help me daily in fulfilling Your plan. Though I have many plans in my heart, I want Your plan to prevail. I don't want to leave anything You've asked of me undone. Change my heart, O God, and make me more like You. In Jesus' Name.

OTHER AREAS OF SUBMISSION

Submit yourselves, then, to God.
(James 4:7)

FROM THE FATHER'S HEART

I've watched you, even while you were being formed in your mother's womb and I've watched you every moment of your life on earth. I loved you from the beginning and love you today. How I long to be with you in eternity. How I long for you to share My heavenly glory. The One who made it possible for us to spend eternity together, My Beloved Son, is coming soon. I love you, My child. How I love you and long to say, "Well done, My good and faithful servant!" Then we will live together in My eternal glory forever and ever.

PERSONAL WORD FROM MY FATHER

Speak, LORD, for your servant is listening.
(1 Samuel 3:9)

ABOUT THE AUTHOR

In addition to being an ordained minister, Therese Marszalek is a dynamic inspirational speaker and author. She has a master's of divinity degree from Shalom Bible College and Seminary and completed Rhema Bible School. Founder of Therese Marszalek Ministries, Therese developed and taught discipleship classes where she finds great joy inspiring others to fulfill their God given destiny. Her message challenges people to walk closer with Christ, yet breathes healing and hope to the discouraged and weary. Her personal experience of searching for Christian truth and longing for a more intimate relationship with Christ birthed her speaking and writing ministry, as well as her zeal for discipleship in the body of Christ. Known for her unique transparency and spiritual depth, Therese draws her audience to a place of vulnerability where God can do His greatest work of transformation. With hundreds of articles in print, as a columnist and contributor to numerous books and television productions, Therese's writing and speaking ministry have reached across the globe to bring a message of hope in Christ.

To contact Therese Marszalek or schedule her for speaking engagements:

Web site: www.theresemarszalek.com

E-mail: therese.marszalek@gmail.com

Or write to: Therese Marszalek Ministries

PO Box 668

Nine Mile Falls, WA 99026

OTHER BOOKS AND GREETING CARD LINE BY THERESE MARSZALEK:

40 Days (Word and Spirit Publishing)

From the Wilderness to the Miraculous (Destiny Image)

Extraordinary Miracles in the Lives of Ordinary People (Harrison House)

Miracles Still Happen (Harrison House)

Breaking Out (Publish America)

The Father's LoveLine greeting card line